SHEMURENGA

.

A note about the title.

In Zimbabwe 'Chimurenga' is commonly associated with the first *chimurenga*, the struggle of the Ndebele and the Shona against colonisation in the late 1800s and the second *chimurenga* the nationalist liberation war waged in the 1960s and 1970s against white minority rule in Rhodesia. The word, as is depicted by these eras speaks to a revolutionary struggle; or popular protest against a set of ideologies, systems and circumstances.

The title of this book **She-murenga** is an attempt to extend and reclaim the word from its dominant meanings. It captures the spirit of struggle against oppressive forces be it for independence, democracy, gender equality, economic justice and ultimately in the context of this book making visible Zimbabwean women's struggles for rights, equality and lives free from violence.

Note: As Fungai Muchirori points out in a conversation in June 2011, the Ndebele equivalent, 'Umvukela Wokuqala', is little quoted in historical and contemporary literature, thus situating this revolutionary concept within Shona language, and I dare add, a predominantly Shona history.

Shereen Essof
December, 2012

SHEMURENGA

The Zimbabwean Women's Movement 1995 – 2000

Shereen Essof

WEAVER
W
—PRESS—

Published by Weaver Press, Box A1922, Avondale, Harare. 2013
<www.weaverpresszimbabwe.com>

Distributed in Europe and the USA by
<www.africanbookscollective.com>

This book was first prepared as a minor dissertation in
partial fulfilment of the requirements for the award of the
degree of Masters of Social Science in Gender and
Transformation, Faculty of Humanities, University of Cape Town, 2003.

Typeset by Weaver Press, Harare
Cover: Danes Design, Harare.
Printed by Preciex, Mauritius

The author and publishers would like to express their grati-
tude to Hivos for the publication of this text.
The contents of this publication are the sole responsibility of the author and do not necessarily represent the views of Hivos.

ISBN: 978-1-77922-214-5

SHEREEN ESSOF is a Zimbabwean feminist, activist, popular educator, and academic. Her academic work is grounded in her engagement with women in trade unions, social movements, and community-based organisations. She strives to understand the roots and the gendered nature of neo-liberal, patriarchal systems, and from that understanding to imagine and organise towards alternatives.

She worked at the Zimbabwe Women's Resource Centre and Network in Harare for six years, and then with the African Gender Institute at the University of Cape Town. At the same time, she has shared her time and capacities with other social justice organisations, not only to strategise, mobilise, and take action but also to create accessible information through oral histories, documentary, creative writing, and art. Shereen has published widely on feminism, women's movements, and social movement organising in both online and hard copy journals in South Africa and internationally.

Currently Shereen leads JASS Southern Africa's programmes on women's rights, empowerment, and movement-building in Malawi, Zambia, and Zimbabwe, and at the regional level. She is known and appreciated for her huge energy and infectious, warm laugh, and for living her feminist principles in everyday life in unpretentious ways.

Contents

Introduction: A Glimpse on the Ground   ix

Chapter 1: Women's Movement Literature: Pushing the Boundaries   1

Chapter 2: Epistemological Tensions Methodological Considerations   8

Chapter 3: The National Context   19

Chapter 4: Zimbabwe Women's Organising 1980-1995   32

Chapter 5: Land, Laws and Votes for Women   43

Chapter 6: Theoretical Challenges; Implications for the Movement   65

Appendices

1. A Snapshot of the Period under Review   83

2. List of Women Conversants   91

3. Bibliography   95

4. The Zimbabwe Women's Charter   101

Introduction

A GLIMPSE ON THE GROUND

On 8 February 2001 representatives from the Zimbabwean Women's Movement gathered at the popular leftist venue, the Book Café, in Harare to try and answer the question: 'Does Zimbabwe have a women's movement?' As the meeting progressed, I became intrigued by the spectrum of views that embodied the debate.

Some questioned whether Zimbabwean women's organising actually constituted a movement and called for a stocktake in quantifying its concrete achievements. Others suggested that the movement had been so weakened ideologically that it was merely propping up and perpetuating the patriarchal status quo that it was trying to overturn. Muted voices recognised a movement but saw it as weak and dismantled.

At the outset I found this deeply problematic. I had lived through some of the most creative and assertive women's rights based organising during the period 1995-2000 when I worked for the Zimbabwean Women's Resource Centre and Network (ZWRCN)[1] and this kind of interrogation seemed to discount and negate my experience.

I knew that the trajectory and terrain of women's organising in Zimbabwe was rich and deep[2] and that women's participation in the nationalist struggle for indepen-

---

1 Based in Harare, Zimbabwe.
2 Traceable to pre-colonial and colonial times. See Schmidt, E. (1992). *Peasants, Traders and Wives: Shona Women in the History of Zimbabwe 1870-1939.* Portsmouth: Heinemann; Barnes, T. (1991). 'Differential Class Experiences Amongst African Women in Colonial Harare, Zimbabwe 1935-1970'. Paper presented at the conference: Women and Gender, University of Natal; Barnes, T. (1999). *'We Women Worked So Hard': Gender, Urbanisation and Social Reproduction in Colonial Harare, Zimbabwe 1930-1956.* Portsmouth: Heinemann.

dence[3] served to provide the impetus for post-independence demands that sought gender equity and disrupted pre-existing gender relations and cultural norms. Initially, the most tangible gains came in the form of legislative change, the most significant of which was the passing of the 1982 Legal Age of Majority Act (LAMA), which saw women being granted majority status at the age of eighteen, paving the way for women's further political and economic empowerment.[4]

On the other hand, patriarchy had reconfigured itself and the political will to meaningfully address gender inequality in Zimbabwe diminished rapidly, being replaced by the desire to regulate and control women both in the private and public sphere. This was done through the very sophisticated and powerful invocation of counter-revolutionary nationalist and cultural discourses that tended to interpolate any women's organising as feminist and feminism as being anti-nationalist, and pro imperialism.

I could site Operation Clean-Up[5] as perhaps the most blatant example of this discursive move, but it was by no means the only one. Another example can be found in the repeated attempts to repeal LAMA, and assert the denial of property and inheritance rights to women under customary law. Yet another example involved the stripping of women who wore mini-skirts in the streets. All these manoeuvres were met by concerted and directed action from women activists: action that was planned in the streets, in offices, around dining-room tables, under trees, and in large city halls.

Furthermore, as Zimbabwe plunged into socio-economic and political upheaval in the late 1990s, the conditions under which women were organising had become increasingly challenging. By this time, the state's unvarnished hostility to gendered discourses meant that women activists became the target of state-sponsored violence. On the other hand the 'deeply uncivil nature of civil society'[6] with regards to gender meant that alliances across sites of struggle, in order to further women's rights based agendas, were tenuous and had to be carefully negotiated.

With this in mind, sitting at the meeting on 8 February, the issue for me was

---

3 Staunton, I. (ed.). 1990. *Mothers of the Revolution*. Harare: Baobab Books.
4 See Appendix 1.
5 Over the weekend of the 28-30 October 1983 when soldiers and police swarmed through the major city centres of Zimbabwe making arbitrary arrests of women. Its purpose was to round-up single women, who were out alone, and charge them with being prostitutes. See Chapter 4.
6 Mama, A. (1999). 'Dissenting Daughters? Gender Politics and Civil Society in a Militarised State'. In CODESRIA Bulletin 3 & 4, p. 31.

not whether or not Zimbabwe had a women's movement. It was more inflected. Instead I found myself asking: given the current national context, what form and shape does a movement have to take in order to survive and deal with the challenges it faces whilst seizing opportunities to further the struggle for gender justice?

Thus, given my positioning as an activist and academic, my aim became two-fold. I wanted to capture the herstory of women's organising in the period 1995-2000, and through this process I sought to develop an analytical understanding, to theorise the movement and its experience of itself as 'weak' and 'fragmented'.

Chapter 1

WOMEN'S MOVEMENT LITERATURE: PUSHING THE BOUNDARIES

Historically, Western feminists largely initiated the contemporary interest and subsequent writing on women's movements in the 1960s.[1] The initial body of work aimed to recover the hidden history of female activism in the North, whilst suggesting that women's political involvement was of a distinctive character and significance. It went on to suggest a somewhat naïve commonality in the forms of women's oppression and women's movements worldwide with its forays into the experiences of women in Southern contexts.

This myth of 'homogenous sisterhood'[2] was soon challenged through the research and writings of Southern feminists. This critique generated a new corpus that shifted the thinking around women's organising in two ways. It highlighted the heterogeneity of women's struggles. It also suggested that in a post-colonial context, women's abilities to form collective identities to articulate their demands are shaped by political processes: these involve shifts in state power, whether they occur through democratic, anti-imperialist or nationalist struggles.[3] Within the trajectory of women's movement literature one has to acknowledge the importance of this re-orientation, and the political message it embodied in chal-

---

1 Rowbotham, S. (1992). *Women in Movement.* New York: Routledge & Kegan Paul.
2 This train of thought prevalent in the 1970s and 1980s is embodied in the concepts underpinning Morgan, R. (1984). *Sisterhood is Global: The International Women's Movement Anthology.* New York: Anchor Press.
3 See, Basu, A. (1995). *The Challenge of Local Feminisms.* Boulder: Westview Press. Mohanty, C. T. et al, (1991). *Third World Women and the Politics of Feminism.* Bloomington: Indiana University Press.

1

lenging Northern hegemony and knowledge production.

Under the rubric of 'third world studies' a body of literature emerged that aimed to explore regional similarities in Africa and elsewhere,[4] but by necessity this leads to the trap of generalisation. As such, this body of work tends to raise more questions than answers as to the particularities of specific contexts and their influence on women's organising and gender politics, thereby outstripping its usefulness. Nonetheless, this perspective did pave the way for deeper contextual case-studies of women's organising, which I will discuss later in this chapter.

Categorisation of Movements

Much time and space has been devoted to categorising women's movements. Many such attempts have drawn from mainstream/malestream social movement theory. This, it can be argued, has obscured the unique features of women's organising, and precluded treating them in their own right. Needless to say there are contrasting views as to what constitutes a movement, but in sum, the literature would suggest that while a movement may be characterised by a diversity of interest, forms of expression and spatial locations, to speak of a movement implies:

> *A social or political phenomenon of some significance, that significance being given by numerical strength, but also capacity to effect change in some way or another be it in legal, cultural, social or political terms.*[5]

This criterion denotes a particular kind of movement, yet, in reality, this is not the only, or even the most important, kind. Sonia Alvarez[6] in her work on Brazil goes a long way in showing forms of 'female collective action' which are, in effect, marked by the absence of one or other of the criteria outlined above. This broader understanding seems more likely to resonate with the diverse manifestation of women's mobilisations in Zimbabwe. Indeed, it is quite possible that the narrow definitions typically found in the literature, which are familiar to Zimbabwean women activists, may have influenced their own conceptions of the movement.

The point I am making is this. If definitional boundaries are going to lock us in and blind us to alternative manifestations of movements and organising, then

---

4   Davies, M. 1983-1987. *Third World – Second Sex: Women's Struggles and National Liberation: Third World Women Speak Out.* London: Zed Press.

5   Molyneux, M. (1998). 'Analysing Women's Movements' in *Development and Change* 29 (2) p. 225.

6   Alvarez, S. (1990). *Engendering Democracy in Brazil: Women's Movements in Transition Politics.* Princeton, NJ: Princeton University Press.

we not only have to ask where the definitions come from and whose interests they serve, but we also have to challenge them, precisely because our lived reality tells us that forms of mobilisation excluded from consideration as 'women's movements' actually make up a large proportion, possibly a greater part, of women's organising and solidarity around the world today. We need to re-claim the term 'movement' and re-define it to our own ends through a process of local critical reflection and engagement with received definitions.

There is also a body of literature, largely generated by the technocratic demands of the development industry, intent on typologising women's organising from community-based welfare organisations and church-based women's interest groups to developmental non-governmental organisations, spanning a range of frameworks from Women in Development (WID), Women and Development (WAD), and Gender and Development (GAD), addressing a range of practical and strategic gender interests.[7] In Zimbabwe, women's organisations can and have been categorised in this way, but to what end?[8] What value does such a categorisation bring to our understanding?

If in the Zimbabwean context the conceptualisation of movements has blinded us to the possibility of recognising our own strength and valuing our organisational forms then categorisation has been operated as a strategy to weaken. It has reinforced the urban = elite = modern = strategic / rural = poor = traditional = practical divide that is manipulated and deployed to weaken and undermine.

In addition, the uptake of these frameworks point to the sophisticated way in which the global development industry has served as a double-edged sword for securing women's rights. It has appropriated politically powerful concepts and used them to its own ends, to facilitate planning and training by 'experts' who are often not versed in the specificities of a context, but are looking for that one recipe which can be applied across the board. In complex ways, language can be used to obscure and water down the critical political edge and dynamism of a movement.

When women's liberation is replaced by 'women in development' or when mobilisation is replaced by 'participation in development', or when political militancy is replaced by lobbying and advocacy skills, ... more than words have been exchanged.

---

7   See: Molyneux, M. (1998). op. cit. Molyneux, M. (1985). 'Mobilisation Without Emancipation? Women's Interests, the State and Revolution in Nicaragua'. *Feminist Issues* 11 (2): 227-253.

8   Jackson, C. & Pearson, R. (1998) *Feminist Visions of Development*. London: Routledge & Kegan Paul. Zwart, G. (1991) 'From WID to GAD More Than a Change in Terminology?' Harare: ZWRCN.

A deal has been done and this has consequences.[9]

I would, however, like to return to the work of Maxine Molyneux[10] who draws on the Nicaraguan experience in her discussion of women's movements. For my purposes her work is of value in that it stretches the boundaries of the literature in the direction in which I would like to move. It was Molyneux who initially applied the concept of women's interests, as drawn from political science, in her 1985 study of *Women's Interests, the State and Revolution in Nicaragua.*[11] She argued against certain constructions of women's interests and critiqued the notion that sex was a sufficient basis for assuming common interests.

The idea of women's interests was diffused into planning contexts through its uptake by the World Bank.[12] This resulted in a rather schematic and simplified model of women's interests that was oblivious to the more nuanced understandings. In a paper largely aimed at a reclamation of the initial dynamism embodied by these concepts, Molyneux combines feminist political theory with development studies, and comes to an understanding of women's movements as 'variant forms of collective action in pursuit of common goals.'[13] She considers the relation of women's movements to 'projects of general political import' be these of an authoritarian or democratic character. Molyneux asserts then that:

> *Discussion of the broader implications of women's politics remains a relatively unexamined aspect of the development literature. There have been some recent attempts to address this absence, yet it is as if the debate within feminist political theory and the field of development studies have pursued parallel paths with little real engagement with each other. This is all the more remarkable given the impact of women's movement on policymaking and politics in the developing world...*[14]

She goes on to explore ways in which contemporary debates about women's movements might be moved on to address the new context that gender politics confronts. In this way she introduces the primacy of the gender politics of a movement as being central to its characterisation.

---

9   Mama, A. (2001). 'Bridging Legacies, Building Futures: Reflecting on African Women's Organisations in the 21st Century'. A paper presented at the Centre for Gender and Organisations Conference, 'Chasms and Differences', Simmonds Centre, Boston, 19-20 June 2001, p. 4.

10 Ibid.

11 Ibid.

12 Moser, C.O.N. (1993). *Gender Planning and Development.* Theory, practice and training. London: Routledge & Kegan Paul.. .

13 Molyneux, M. (1998) p. 219.

14 Ibid.

This, then, is something worth holding on to, especially in the struggle for a transformatory feminist politics. Within the context of the development industry it is easy to parade a technocratic gender discourse, but if male authority is taken for granted and left intact, then this is a different way of seeing the world to that which evolves in the course of a transformatory feminist politics. Given the heterogeneity of our contexts and movements this is something we must of necessity keep in the frame.

Literature on Women's Movements in Africa

To inflect the discussion by turning to Africa, one finds sophisticated forms of organising undertaken by women on the continent. Whether it be Ugandan women securing a 30 per cent quota for representation in parliament, Nigerian women holding Chevron-Texaco hostage until it agreed to fulfil its promises of schools, electrical and water systems or Zimbabwean women fighting for the installation of a woman chief, much more is happening on the ground than is being written about.

If we turn to those writings focusing on African women's organising, from Nina Mba's pioneering 1982 study[15] onwards, there has been a growing body of work focussing on African women's movements: their organising and participation in national socio-economic and political processes on the continent.[16] These studies do not, by any means, add up to a comprehensive picture of women's movements in Africa. Rather, they attempt to grapple with the specificities and the profound diversity within our particular social movements and contexts, providing a platform from which to build and develop subsequent questions for further research in an attempt to deepen our knowledge base of women's organ-

15 Mba, N. (1982). *Nigerian Women Mobilized: Women's Political Activity in Southern Nigerian, 1900-1965*. Berkeley: Institute of International Studies at the University of California in Berkeley.

16 And here I am referring to the works of for example: Badran, M. (1996). *Feminists, Islam and Nation: Gender and the Making of Modern Egypt*. Cairo: Cairo University Press; Lazreg, M. (1994). *The Eloquence of Silence: Algerian Women in Question*. London: Routledge & Kegan Paul; Tsikata, E. (1989). 'Women in Political Organisations 1951-1987' in Hansen, E. & Ninsink, K. (eds). *The State and Development and Politics in Ghana*. Dakar: CODESRIA; Manuh, T. (1993). 'Women, the State and Society under the PNDC' in Gyimah-Boadi. E. (ed) *Ghana Under PNDC Rule*. Dakar: CODESRIA; Manuh, T. (1991). 'Women and their Organisations during the CPP Period' in Arhin, K. (ed). *The Life and Work of Kwame Nkrumah*. Accra: SEDCO. Tamale, S. (1999). *When Hens Begin To Crow: Parliamentary Politics in Uganda*. Boulder: Westview Press; Tripp, A. M. (2000). *Women in Politics in Uganda*. Oxford: James Currey; Geiger, S. (1998). *TANU Women: Gender and Culture in the Making of Tanganyikan Nationalism*. Oxford: James Currey.

ising on the continent.

The one thing, however, that this work attests to unequivocally is the centrality of the state in women's organising in Africa,[17] highlighting a relationship that is somewhat contradictory. On the one hand, the state is regarded as patriarchal, repressive and excluding, on the other, women's advocacy involves demanding an expansion in the roles of the state through the provision of services and the establishment of frameworks that mitigate gendered impacts and ensure gender equality. As Tsikata[18] points out:

> ...*Analysis has shown that state action is often both gender-blind and gender-biased, both independent and state-sponsored activists have sought to rely solely on the state to outlaw gender discrimination, with limited success.*

There is no doubt that this kind of scenario would present opportunities, risks and tensions or what Vargas refers to as 'contradictions and deficits'.[19] To site one example: equality mechanisms for Zimbabwean women may have been broadened through the state's engagement with global standards of democracy and rights[20] but, at the same time, these possibilities depend on the socio-economic and political interests of the state in furthering its own agenda.

Thus, I would like to argue that like the development industry, the state too becomes a double-edged sword for women. On the one hand it is a powerful tool for the production of equality but, on the other, a source for the reproduction of inequality, depending on its own agenda in securing and maintaining legitimacy and power. Further, the literature shows women's understanding of the nature of the state profoundly shapes the form and content of activism and gender politics.

This being said, Amina Mama challenges us to confront the reality that the work on women's movements in Africa continues to be largely Northern in scope, orientation and voice. She goes further to suggest that the muted presence of African women's scholarship continues to reflect deep global inequalities, as resources and power remain rooted in the North and often the agenda for study is dictated by Western interests, which may go some way in explaining:

17 Tsikata, D. (1999). 'Gender Equality and the State in Ghana: Some Issues of Policy and Practice'. In Imam, A. et al. *Engendering African Social Sciences.* Dakar: CODESRIA. Mama, A. (1999). 'Dissenting Daughters? Gender Politics and Civil Society in a Militarised State' in CODESRIA Bulletin 3 & 4.

18 Tsikata, D. op. cit. p. 382.

19 Vargas, V. (1991). 'The Women's Movement in Peru: Streams, Spaces and Knots' in *European Review of Latin American and Caribbean Studies,* 50, pp. 7-50.

20 See CEDAW, which Zimbabwe ratified in 1991, or the 1995 Beijing Platform for Action.

The persistent tolerance we have for simplification and misunderstanding of African women's organisations, the rationales that lead them to organise, and indeed the strategic acumen and effectiveness that many of them have displayed, often under extremely challenging conditions.[21]

Research Question

I have tried to show through a survey of the literature on women's movements that currently the field has limited applicability and it lacks an empirical research base. I see elements of my experience of the movement in Zimbabwe refracted in many ways and thus the literature has served to provide very broad brush strokes of the terrain I find myself in.

A comprehensive continental picture of women's organising would allow for more of a dialogic exploration, but in the absence of this, this research project aims to add to the continental case study material while traversing the boundaries of the literature in order to allow me to fully 'see' women's organising and the women's movement in Zimbabwe for what it is. This is both frustrating and exciting. Frustrating because of the limited nature of the conceptual tools available for this work, exciting because my task will involve pushing the limits of the theory through a detailed exploration of the praxis developed in one particular and rapidly changing context.

My experience and current positioning facilitates this, as I am part of the Zimbabwean women's movement but I am also taking advantage of an intellectually supportive feminist environment, which recognises the importance of African women's writings and allows for the reflective space and time to do just that. It is from this somewhat unique positioning that I take up the challenge of examining the women's movement in Zimbabwe. My research will be framed by the question: what are the major challenges and opportunities that have faced the movement during the period 1995-2000, and how has it navigated these?

---

21 Mama, A. (2001) op. cit.

Chapter 2

EPISTEMOLOGICAL TENSIONS
METHODOLOGICAL CONSIDERATIONS

I have already illustrated the paucity of a comprehensive literature on women's organising in a post-colonial context. Thus it is expedient and easy to make the urgent call for more work on women in Africa, by African women, to serve our agendas. But what are the epistemological and methodological challenges in operationalising this call?

Clearly, from my research experience, they cannot be anticipated. They are revealed as the process unfolds, manifesting in various ways and presenting multiple challenges. During these challenging moments my instinct was to turn to the literature in search of spirit guides, the writings and reflections on process that would assist me in addressing the challenges of my findings by equipping me with the conceptual tools or at the very least inspiring me to go on. But while I scanned the literature for self-reflexive works, I rapidly discovered that work of this nature is a rarity.

If we are to commit to developing feminist research capacity on this continent, then I firmly believe that we need to engage in the necessary critical reflection that surfaces the challenges that underpin feminist research in Africa. I would argue that reflections on process and strategy need to be reinstated and undertaken with a deeper understanding of the importance of knowledge production as a powerful tool in challenging patriarchy and western hegemony. In this chapter my intention is to do just this. I aim to reflect on my own research experience through a discussion of methodology and feminist research tools in an attempt to begin conversations that articulate the challenges that underpin feminist research on the continent.

Standpoint Theory and Situated Knowledges

Within the positivist paradigm the position of the researcher is generally left inviolate. Feminists, however, have argued that it is necessary to make the researcher visible in order to understand the epistemological process: how and why knowledge is produced. One of my central challenges in this research project is located at this juncture: coming to terms with my own position as a 'knowledge producer'.

The underlying aim of feminist standpoint theory,[22] as derived from Marxism and as a critique of positivist approaches,[23] is to bring those at the margins into the centre through the creation and acknowledgement of a multiplicity of voices and the need for oppressed groups to re-claim for themselves the value of their own experience. Standpoint theory suggests that knowledge is inescapably position-bound, hence both partial and partisan in character. It suggests that differing positions within society create a system of dualisms that privilege some people while devaluing others. In this context, marginalised groups work to understand not only their own standpoints, but also the underlying structures of the dominant standpoint as their survival hinges upon an acquired ability to communicate and participate in the dominant discourse.[24]

One of the fascinating insights emanating from this theory is the idea that the oppressed may cultivate an 'epistemic advantage'[25] from having knowledge of the practices of both their own contexts and those of their oppressors. This advantage is thought to lead to critical insights because it provokes critical perspectives. Taking this train of thought to its logical conclusion means that systems of dominance and power can be undermined and subverted as a result of the 'dual knowledge of the oppressed' or the ability to operate in two different

---

22 Feminist standpoint theorists make three principal claims: (1) Knowledge is socially situated. (2) Marginalised groups are socially situated in ways that make it more possible for them to be aware of certain issues, and ask questions about them, than it is for the non-marginalised. (3) Research, particularly that focused on power relations, should begin with the lives of the marginalised. Therefore feminist standpoint theories place relations between political and social power, and knowledge centre-stage.

23 See Hartsock, N. (1983). 'The Feminist Standpoint' in Harding, S. & M. B. Hintikka (eds). *Discovering Reality: Feminist Perspectives on Epistemology, Metaphysics, Methodology and Philosophy of Science*. Dordrecht: Reidel. Harding, S. (1995). 'Strong Objectivity: A Response to the New Objectivity Question' in *Synthesis*, 104 (3),

24 This same pressure does not exist for the dominant group, due to their historical legitimacy.

25 Narayan, U. (1989). 'The Project of Feminist Epistemology: Perspectives From a Non-Western Feminist' in Jagger, A. and Bordo, S. (eds). *Gender/Body/Knowledge: Feminist Reconstructions of Being and Knowing*. New Brunswick: Rutgers University Press.

contexts with two sets of practices. This dual knowledge is supposed to allow for the understanding of hostile terrains and the employment of strategies to advance struggles for justice.

At one level the underlying aims of standpoint theory converged with my own interests to document and reinstate a herstory. At another it raised serious and debilitating questions precisely around my own positioning[26] and what constitutes a credible standpoint. I was committed to minimising the power differentials in my research relationship[27] because I believed that the herstory needed to be narrated by the voices of 'Zimbabwean women', the voices who had a right to lay claim to the herstory. I had unconsciously invested in an 'authentic'[28] voice and, in doing so, I negated and elided my own experience through a refusal to engage with the power I had as a knowledge producer, to select and define.

To this end, I saw my role as that of a channel or facilitator in documenting a shared herstory. My commitment was to level the research playing field to the extent that research participants, many of whom carried a longer history than myself, would inform research process and analysis.[29] Needless to say, I soon began to comprehend the impossibility of what I was seeking to do. For example, early on in my research,[30] I found that the conversants' immediate reality was so pressing that it did not necessarily allow for the luxury of time or space for critical reflection to enable this much talked about 'epistemic advantage'. I discovered that women's heterogeneity meant that there was no one version of the herstory of the movement, and as a result, neither could there be a shared authorial voice.

I had, in fact, fallen into the exact same trap that I am going to suggest befell the movement.[31] I had failed to critically address its heterogeneity and my own identity and positioning. I had not considered the impact which this would have on a research process intended to produce a herstory.[32] I realised that in order to move forward, I needed to explore the 'dark side' to the 'double vision' of standpoint theory sometimes perhaps uncritically advanced, as the answer to

26 See below.
27 Which is important in and of itself.
28 Voices that were of the vanguard – female and black. See McFadden, P. (2000). 'The State of Feminism in Africa Today'. *Commentaries*, Nordic Africa Institute (2).
29 This was reflected in my initial methodological considerations, which focussed on conversations with women activists and focus group discussions in order to collectively analyse the data emphasising a commitment to shared process.
30 During the conversations with women activists.
31 See Chapter 4.
32 Interestingly, this impasse manifested itself through a loss of voice and an inability to write coherently about the movement.

the problem of their own hegemony among women, by our Northern counterparts.[33]

To do this I turned to Uma Narayan[34] who suggests that the enterprise of feminist epistemology poses broader political problems for 'non-western' feminists because, amongst other controversies including false universalism, epistemic relativism and the bias paradox[35], feminist epistemology fails to take cognisance of the inflections of the post-colonial subject: inflections that have the potential to unfurl into multiple identities and positionings thereby complicating the notion of a standpoint.

I realised that I needed to reclaim my voice through an examination of my own positioning within the movement. I am a feminist, a woman, of south Indian descent with an ancestry that intersects with European and African traditions. I am Zimbabwean, yet I may not be considered such because I am not regarded as 'fully' black or 'fully' African by many Zimbabweans. My body represents a certain race, class and politics which I have to continually deconstruct. What epistemic advantage, if any, does *my* position afford *me*?

In the first instance, my mix of identities means that I have learned the ability to operate with a certain degree of accomplishment across diverse social and racial contexts. I can manoeuvre myself and navigate through varied cultural, social and political terrains. At any one time I can be both an 'insider' and 'outsider'. Significantly, however, I realise that it is not my identity but my work within the movement that translates to belonging. The history that I carried meant that I was welcomed back, supported and affirmed in my research process. 'First, I want to say how pleased I am that you are doing this valuable work. It must be done.'[36]

---

33 Since feminist standpoint theory argues that enquiry is best started from women's lives, and that standpoints emerge only when women begin to reflect upon and question the reality of those lives through a politicised framework, this theory can be misunderstood as proposing a single (essentialised) fundament. This is further compounded when the standpoint is presented as arising from ordinary women's lives but has, in fact, been mediated through the lens of relatively privileged, mostly middle-class, mostly white, female academics.

34 Narayan, U. (1998) op. cit.

35 It is claimed that there is no standpoint-neutral vantage point from which to make judgements about the relative epistemic superiority of certain standpoints over other ways of knowing the world; while on the other hand, it is claimed that marginalised standpoints are, indeed, epistemically better than the epistemic positions of the non-marginalised. If this tension cannot be resolved, it is argued, the standpoint theorist is pushed back towards the relativistic embrace of 'multiple and incompatible knowledge positions'..

36 Conversant transcript.

But I also realise that 'belonging' is an unstable category. The state's orchestrated race war in Zimbabwe means that while I have found a space within the movement as a feminist activist, my position is precarious. I can become an outsider as the politics of nationalism destabilises my self as a category within a movement that has not spent adequate time discussing issues of difference. Currently, too, I am distanced from the movement in my role as analyst, based at the University of Cape Town.[37] The reflective pedagogic space this affords provides a means for my own sense-making and analysis, a space that I found to be affirmed and valued by the movement:

> *...The space to think and reflect is a valuable thing. I think we need it, that's one of the things that's been missing; we need to have some of our members going and coming back, sharing their experience, to enable us to answer the question, are we getting it right?*[38]

Only by coming to terms with my own identity, positioning and the contribution I was making as a feminist activist and analyst was I able to meaningfully complete this piece of work. The relationship between the sites I inhabit is not simple and straightforward. In fact, inhabiting multiple contexts whilst maintaining a critical edge incurs a certain price: varying degrees of rootlessness and alienation, belonging nowhere and everywhere.

Thus, I do not claim a standpoint per se; neither do I claim an epistemic advantage. I am working in the terrain of situated knowledges. The diverse spaces I inhabit are not about individuals with the same identities coming together, nor about a notion of a single woman and women's experience, rather it is about individuals – with a common vision rooted in the political – coming together to form conscious coalitions, or what Chela Sandoval[39] terms 'oppositional consciousness' in describing those individuals who become, for whatever reasons... 'Skilled in reading webs of power as a result of their unstable membership in social categories'.

Thus I present my work as a critical engagement with my context, the research site and myself. This groundbreaking study yields a perspective on my world, the world of the Zimbabwe women's movement, as I have been able to view, research and document it.

---

37 In 2003/4.
38 Conversant transcript.
39 Haraway uses Chela Sandoval's term, p. 156. See Haraway, D. (1991). *Simians, Cyborgs, and Women: The Reinvention of Nature*. New York: Routledge & Kegan Paul.

Research Strategy: the Case Study

If feminist epistemology is concerned with bringing those at the margins into the centre through a reclaiming, reinstating and valuing of women's experience, then what better way to elicit the experiences of women's organising than through the building of a case study. Case studies are a tool of feminist research and their value lies in defying generalisations through the quest for specificity. This I believe coincides with my aim of looking at a particular movement within its particular context.

This case, therefore, maps the development of the Zimbabwean women's movement during the period 1995-2000. The literature has already pointed to the inter-relationship between women's movements and national process. Thus I aimed to track the trajectory of the movement alongside national socio-economic and political developments taking place in and across broader Zimbabwean society. A period in history cannot be read in isolation from what has preceded it, thus the period pre-1995 and post-2000 are described to provide the context for more recent events.

I soon realised that it would be necessary for me to 'claim facts', to describe the national context and background to women's organising (Chapters 3 and 4) and present this as a methodological pivot in order to fully explore the women's movement in the period under review (Chapters 5 and 6). I welcome challenges to my choices of the sequencing and privileging of certain events over others.

Building the Case

I found that this research process had, in fact, been eight years in the making and my own experience, once reinstated, formed the backbone upon which I fleshed out the case.[40] To do this I chose qualitative research methods,[41] which allowed me to gather an extensive range of primary and secondary data responding to the specific circumstances of my research project, whilst creating room for innovation and creativity where necessary.

Open-ended Conversations

The first thing I did once I had arrived in Zimbabwe was schedule appointments

---

40 I visited Zimbabwe with the specific intention of undertaking fieldwork for this project in May 2001, and stayed in Zimbabwe through July of that same year, a period which spanned the June 2001 parliamentary elections.
41 There is a non-existence of baseline data on women or gender disaggregated statistics.

for conversations with women activists.[42] This 'purposive sample' was selected as representative[43] of interest groups within the movement and included: gender activists working in urban and rural areas, feminists, women working within women's rights orientated organisations, as independent consultants, within government structures, and within the academy. They reflected a racial and a generational spread, which it was hoped would texture and enrich the data, providing a nuanced perspective of events along a time continuum.

Zimbabwe is a fertile location for researchers, especially from the North, and inherent tensions accrue. With a profusion of requests, already burdened organisations and individuals become guarded regarding what their participation implies in a research process that is not their own. Further, research is often jeopardised by fettered access to a research site.

> *I get people coming in all the time … Why give so much of yourself, they take and take and in the end you have nothing left. They come and they go and you never gain the benefits from the research undertaken. So we're very happy to have Zimbabweans doing this kind of work because there is so little.*[44]

My positioning meant that the series of gatekeepers who would ordinarily 'protect' organisational integrity and memory, melted away. As previously mentioned, my commitment to minimising the power differentials in my research process led me to choose open-ended conversations which I believed was a more equal process than that defined by the rigid relationship of interviewer and researched.

The method sought historical narratives through the use of a 'critical moment technique'. Prior knowledge of these women meant that my entry point was through a discussion of a particular event or moment within the history that they could provide insight into. This, then, led to conversations exploring broader issues pertinent to the movement.

In total, I conducted sixteen conversations.[45] They all lasted in the region of an hour and a half. I engaged with the selected women wherever they were at, literally and figuratively, in acknowledgement of the pressures bearing down upon them. Thus conversations were held at places of work both within and outside

---

42 All of these women were colleagues, some were friends. See Appendix 2 and 3.

43 The scope of the project mitigated against broad-based consultations with women. As a researcher I am aware of the privileging of certain voices over others. For a list of women interviewed see Appendix 3.

44 Conversant transcript.

45 On average 3-4 per week.

the home, in cars, hotels, over meals, some conversations even rolled out into consecutive days. All the conversations were recorded and fully transcribed. This process yielded 120 pages of transcript, single-spaced 10 pt typeface. Notes were not taken during the conversations as this was too distracting and I experienced it as contrived.

For purposes of confidentiality and safety I have chosen not to directly attribute quotations to particular women. Rather I have chosen to refer to these women as 'conversants', a term that I believe reflects the conversational nature of data acquisition.

The method produced non-standardised information that allowed full use of differences amongst the women. It provided snapshots of moments in time and allowed me to access the ideas, thoughts and memories of women in their own words, which was refreshing. But more than this, the technique involved a cumulative knowledge building process. It unfurled a mosaic of a herstory as the conversations began to mingle, layer and resonate with each other. Concerns and understandings began to emerge, all versions of key events and articulations of possible meanings.

This method had unexpected outcomes. In some instances, the conversations acted as catalysts for deeper thinking and reflection both on the part of myself as the researcher and the conversants. The process laid bare the tensions that accrue for women who are committed to a cause and the costs that they incur in the form of being overstretched. In numerous instances the meetings provided much needed reflective space for the women activists I was in conversation with: 'I'd love a copy of this tape, because you are really stimulating me to think about things.'[46]

But they also highlight the value of reflection in order to inform new directions and activism.

I found this conversation very interesting, I actually have the time to reflect and it's interesting, it's raising things I'd never thought of, things that need to be considered in developing plans and strategies.[47]

Participant Observation

Simply being in Zimbabwe provided a rich source of data. I began to tap into the immense energy and excitement being generated as the parliamentary elections

---

46 Conversant transcript.
47 Conversant transcript.

drew closer and the possibility for change hovered in the air. For the first time in twenty years ZANU-PF appeared to have a consolidated opposition in the form of the Movement for Democratic Change and the change in the balance of power became real.

> *The discourse of change is everywhere. Despair and hope exist side by side and activists are caught between the polarities, sometimes immobilised by them. The struggle ahead is overwhelming, yet people still believe in the ability to see the present through to a better future ... everywhere there is a feeling of transition and flux.*[48]

Activists resorted to social engagement and activity by night as an escape from the intense and increasingly dangerous work being done during the day. My research process enmeshed with the rhythms of life and extended into intense evenings of socialising, conversation and analysis about the Zimbabwean context, civil society's role in the process of social change and the positioning of the women's movement. Thus the research experience became organic, invigorating and enriching.

> *...Days are busy but nights seem to be even busier. Evenings spent at the Italian Bakery, the Book Café unroll fervent analysis and debate about the current scenario.*[49]

By necessity, people created the time and space to reflect and confer on the exacting circumstances being faced in Zimbabwe. Every person I met and every conversation I had contributed to a greater understanding of the Zimbabwean women's movement and/or its context. I could never quite anticipate where the next interesting insight would come from or in what form it would be embodied: armed, however, with a notebook, I was able to capture some of these debates and gather material that ordinarily would have been inaccessible.

As my fieldwork progressed, however, information gaps in my knowledge base began to surface. The first of these emerged around my intention to plot events in the women's movement against broader national processes. I realised that in order to undertake this task comprehensively, I needed to develop a map of broad national socio-economic and political processes in the period under review. The second arose in relation to filling my own information gaps regarding the women's movement, details of its activities and processes.

Published Material

Being on familiar terrain I knew what kinds of information I needed and where

---

48 Field journal entry 24 May 2001.
49 Ibid.

I would find it. Accessing published material was fairly straightforward. I had a good idea of the limited range of published literature in existence and within that what I needed. I also knew that much of this material was available at the Zimbabwe Women's Resource Centre (ZWRCN) and Network library, which has a comprehensive collection of local, regional and international gender and development resources.

Organisational Publications

Organisational publications on conference proceedings, reports, published civic education material as well as research reports deepened my own understanding and appreciation of the national context, civil society[50] and the women's movement[51] in Zimbabwe.

Unpublished Material

With regards to unpublished material, I was clear about what existed because I had lived this period. The path to access it, however, was more complicated. My strategy eventually became one of negotiation in order to peruse organisational archives. It is a risky and invasive strategy because its success is dependent on already fragile organisations laying themselves open. It was a strategy I employed precisely because I knew I was trusted[52] and my colleagues were willing to oblige and facilitate the process whilst uppermost in my mind was the honouring of the trust and confidences that people and organisations imbibed in me.

Newspaper Scan

I concentrated on two newspapers, *The Herald*, which is a daily paper commonly understood to be state-controlled, and the *Zimbabwe Independent*, which as its name suggests, is an independently owned weekly paper. Both papers agreed for me to access their archives. So, I spent numerous hours in dusty corners scanning papers in order to identify and plot chronologically the trajectory of national debates and happenings. This process largely supported the development of the tables.[53]

---

50 See for example: Moyo, S., Makumbe, J. and Raftopoulos, B. (2000). *NGOs, the State and Politics in Zimbabwe*. Harare: SAPES.

51 See for example: Staunton, I. (1990). op. cit; Getecha, C. & Chipika, J. (1995). *Zimbabwe Women's Voices*. Harare: ZWRCN; Watson, P. (1998). *Determined to Act*. Harare. WAG; Tichagwa, W. (1998). *Beyond Inequalities: Women in Zimbabwe*. Harare: SARDC/ZWRCN.

52 Something that I value and respect and will not violate.

53 See Appendix 1.

I was also granted access to the ZWRCN newspaper cutting collection, which documents and highlights gender issues and their reporting in Zimbabwe. This collection allowed me to assess not only what the gender debates focused around in the period under review, but also how women's organising impacted upon national consciousness.

Organisation minutes and internal reports

Noting the paucity of published materials on the women's movement in Zimbabwe and the 'snapshots' of the movement being elicited through the conversations, I realised that I would need to rely on unpublished materials to further flesh out my mapping of the movement. This material took the form of minutes and reports of strategic meetings held within the movement, internal organisational documentation and correspondence around events and campaigns, lobbying and advocacy campaign materials.[54] I also undertook a broad scan of women's rights, gender and development and feminist organisations in Zimbabwe in order to develop organisational profiles of the kinds of organising being undertaken within the movement.

Research Journal

During the entire period of the research process: conceptualisation, fieldwork and write-up I kept a research journal. This provided a means for me to monitor my own feelings, and thoughts on the research topic and process. I include it as data in order to further illustrate my commitment to self-reflexivity.

---

54 For this I am indebted to the ZWRCN, The Women's Coalition Secretariat, The NCA, and MWENGO.

Chapter 3

THE NATIONAL CONTEXT

My research unfolded against the backdrop of one of the most trying and exciting times in the history of post-independent Zimbabwe. Towards the middle of my research process, I found myself writing:

> *Zimbabwe is a truly beautiful place going through 'harsh economic times'. The reality of this very common sound bite translates into a nightmare of harrowing proportions. One witnesses the infrastructure crumbling little by little: potholes appear on the streets, they get bigger. No one fixes them. Traffic lights and street signs disappear to be melted down or sold. Shortages of petrol means queues can snake for kilometres around petrol stations, people waiting for hours and days in the hope of getting fuel. HIV/AIDS related deaths soar out of control. The plummeting Zimbabwean dollar means that the 'alternative economy' has proliferated; prices in the markets go up dramatically every other day, while the expectation for something to oil the wheels results in wide-spread corruption. The prevailing political culture has eroded shared meanings and this has resulted in polarisation. While undemocratic practice and manipulation of the rule of law speak succinctly to the fact that politicians do what they think is necessary and what will keep them in power on the day, Zimbabwean people are engaged in the game of survival and scapegoats come in many forms including the female. You cannot hide from the state of flux and uncertainty; it meets you at every corner and is echoed in every conversation. The dominant questions include 'is a post nationalist politics propelled by progressive currents on the horizon? Has the fatigue associated with ZANU's malgovernance and economic mistakes finally reached breaking point? Will the MDC, the new labour party emerge as the organisational base for popular aspirations in the July 2000 parliamentary elections.*[55]

55 Field Journal Entry 1 June 2001.

In sum, this context formed a potent cocktail of dashed hopes, social desperation and economic fall-out coupled with a new consciousness and options for social resistance. But let us take a step back to unpack and trace the underpinnings of this current scenario.

Zimbabwe's independence was ushered in 1980 after years of colonial rule, a protracted *chimurenga*, or war for liberation, and hard bargaining, which eventually resulted in the Lancaster House Agreement of 1979.[56] This British-brokered agreement called for a ceasefire, new elections, a transition period under British rule and a new constitution implementing majority rule. Yet the indecisive military victory of the two major parties, the largely Shona Zimbabwe African National Union (ZANU) led by Robert Mugabe and the majority Ndebele Zimbabwe African People's Union (ZAPU), led by Joshua Nkomo, as well as nationalist infighting leading up to the Lancaster House negotiations, left various kinds of residual economic and political power in white minority hands.

At independence, Zimbabwe had a sound economic base, with the advantage of high levels of entrepreneurial talent and general human capital, which allowed for import substitution. In the first two years of independence GDP growth rate was a spectacular 21 per cent,[57] as a result of good rains, the removal of economic and travel sanctions, and a return of Zimbabwe to international legitimacy; all of which led to more confidence amongst investors in the economy and the growth in consumer power.

Under the leadership of ZANU's[58] Robert Mugabe, the 1980s were committed to a socialist development agenda of national reconciliation and reconstruction. During this period, the state's priorities were to integrate the armed forces,[59] re-establish social services, including health and education in rural areas, and re-settle, as a result of the war of liberation, the estimated one million refugees and displaced persons, whilst committing to reversing past discriminatory policies in, for example, land distribution, and employment practice.

Within the first decade, the state and the ruling party became indistinguishable. A lower-middle class was quickly built through the bureaucracy, and a pa-

---

56 See: 1980. Report of the Constitutional Conference Lancaster House London September – December 1979. London: Her Majesty's Stationary Office. Available at: http://wanadoo.nl/rhodesia/lanc1.html

57 *Zimbabwe Economic Review*, 1999.

58 The first independent elections saw Robert Mugabe's ZANU gaining a majority of 62%, ZAPU getting 24%, and the collaborating black party just 8% with a voter turnout of 95%.

59 The armed wings were known as ZANLA and ZIPRA respectively. At independence the two forces had to merge into one army, together with the Rhodesian National Army.

tronage system that ran contrary to the state's socialist and egalitarian goals. As a left-wing ZANU MP, concluded in 1989:

> *The socialist agenda has been adjourned indefinitely. You don't talk about social-*
> *ism in a party that is led by people who own large tracts of land and employ a lot of*
> *cheap labour. When the freedom fighters were fighting in the bush they were fighting*
> *not to disturb the system but to dismantle it. And what are we seeing now? Leaders*
> *are busy implementing those things which we were fighting against.*[60]

During this time too, ethnic dominance of the state by the Shona generated resentment by the minority Ndebeles. ZANU's distinctive coercive strain manifested in independent Zimbabwe when the 5th Brigade, comprised largely of Shona-speaking members of the armed wing of ZANU, standing outside of the army chain of command, and answering only to Mugabe himself unleashed the Gukurahundi (the early rain which washes away the chaff before the spring rains), the regime's first, and still unpunished, genocide.

While an accurate death toll for the Gukurahundi is all but impossible to ascertain, it is safe to say that over 5,000 people were killed and displaced by the 5th Brigade, the ZANU-PF Youth Militia, the Central Intelligence Organisation (CIO), and the Police Internal Security Intelligence Unit (PISI).[61]

This violent coercion ultimately culminated in the 1987 unity pact between Mugabe's ZANU and Nkomo's ZAPU resulting in a merger between the two parties and the birth of the Zimbabwe African National Union – Patriotic Front (ZANU-PF). This set the stage for what was to become a de facto one-party state. ZANU-PF's efforts to codify this into law were beaten back not only by human rights advocates, but also by international opinion, at a time when Zimbabwe sought more access to global markets.

Internally, through the 1980s, the power of financial institutions grew, reflecting the growing stagnation of local manufacturing, and a desperate search for external markets to counteract this. Very high levels of foreign debt[62] were followed by a reduced capacity to control the economy from the vantage point of the nation-state. Thus the early 1990s witnessed domestic financial markets imploding, as international interests gained dominance in the local economy and

---

60 *The Sunday Mail,* 10 December 1989.

61 See *Breaking the Silence Building True Peace A Report on the 1980s Disturbances in Matabeleland the Midlands 1980 to 1988.* Catholic Commission for Justice and Peace in Zimbabwe and The Legal Resources Foundation, Harare. 1997.

62 The balance of payments situation deteriorated from a surplus of US$41.9 million at independence to a deficit of US$120 million in 1989.

successfully removed trade and financial restrictions. All the above had the effect of sinking Zimbabwe into a profound economic depression further exacerbated by the 1992 drought. This interesting blend of ingredients had implications for Zimbabwe's economy as the creeping policy influence by the International Monetary Fund (IMF) and the World Bank (WB) was transformed into outright coercion to adopt economic structural adjustment (ESAP) under the premise that the adoption of this policy reform was considered compatible with the contemporary style of sustainable national economic development.

Economic Structural Adjustment

With the introduction of ESAP in 1990,[63] Zimbabwe moved to privatise state enterprises and liberalise the economy, eliminate price subsidies on basic commodities; slash government expenditure, open domestic markets to foreign investors through the reduction of restrictions and provision of lucrative concessions, deregulate currency and financial markets in the name of achieving export competitiveness; institute 'cost recovery' for education, health care, and other social services and increase cash exports to reduce foreign debts.

This coupled with growing nepotism, corruption and mismanagement amounted to backtracking on independence promises, and the trade-offs resulted in further deterioration. By 1995 the IMF and WB began to apply greater pressure for 'compliance' and a balance-of-payments support tranche of Z$620 million was withheld.[64]

During this period one saw an erosion of the social development and progress of the early 1980s.[65] The elimination of price controls on manufactured goods, retrenchment of workers, devaluation of currency and privatisation of government industries resulted in a sharp shrinkage of income opportunities for the urban-middle and working class while simultaneously marginalising the poor further, to the extent that even perceived urban opportunities for the rural poor were eroded. Further, the reduction of social welfare and the disappearance of free or subsidised access to health and education meant that these rights were

63 See World Bank (1987). *Zimbabwe: A Strategy for Sustained Growth*.
64 See 'Minister Fears Donors Could Ape World Bank Example'. The *Financial Gazette*, 29 February 1996. In fact the suspension of aid from the IMF did result in other donors withholding aid; for example, the European Union announced in March 1996 that it would give Zimbabwe US$32 million for drought relief, health and education, but would block disbursements until IMF/World Bank conditions, and specifically fiscal targets were met
65 See UNDP (1999). Human Development Report: Globalisation with a Human Face. Zimbabwe. http://hdr.undp.org/reports/detail_reports.cfm?view=598

seriously eroded and lost their power to placate. In 1995, with mass retrenchments and joblessness, poverty increased dramatically and the hunger for land
began to grow, as oft-repeated redistribution promises by the government came
to nought.

In the wake of 8% GDP growth in 1996 and 3% in 1997 and a national debt
of US$37 billion,[66] the dangers of Zimbabwe's quite advanced financial liberali-
sation were starkly unveiled when in one day, over a few hours,[67] the Zimbabwe
dollar fell by 75%, requiring a temporary central bank bailout and reassertion
of currency controls just to raise the exchange rate to half its previous value.
Inflation rose from levels below 15% in September 1997 to above 45% eighteen
months later, with far higher price increases recorded for food. Newspapers report that more than 30,000 jobs were lost through retrenchments during 1998,
as economic growth barely cleared 1%.

Two political events in late 1997 attract blame for Zimbabwe's meltdown.
First, Robert Mugabe silenced nearly 50,000 liberation war veterans who challenged his legitimacy by granting them Z$50,000 each,[68] plus a pension of
Z$2,000 per month.[69] It is argued that the ex-combatants were successful be-
cause their demonstrations in Harare caused the ZANU-PF government acute
embarrassment and threatened its power bases due to its failure to deliver on
promises dating back almost two decades. After the payout, however, intense
popular resentment against the war vets emerged, as sales taxes and an income
tax and petrol tax increase were imposed to help cover the costs.

Second, in September 1998, after a round table donor conference, Mugabe
announced that, at long last, the government would begin implementing the
1993 Land Designation Act.

Land

At the time of independence approximately 6,000 white farmers[70] owned over
50% of Zimbabwe's most fertile farmland, while in Communal Areas, 700,000
families occupied less than 50% of the least fertile agricultural land.[71] Despite

---

66 The *Financial Gazette*, 11 January 1997.
67 14 November 1997, also known as Black Friday.
68 US $2,800 at the time.
69 The *Financial Gazette*, 'Huge Pay-Outs for Ex-fighters'. 28 August 1997. *Financial Gazette*, 'The
   High Price of Peace and Folly'. 4 September 1997.
70 2% of the population. See The *Mail and Guardian*, 'Zimbabwe Focus: Racism Lingers, but
   Class Divides'. 3 March 1999.
71 As above.

these inequities, the terms of the Lancaster House Constitution ensured limited transformation within the sector. Within the parameters of this constitution, expropriation of private property was prohibited and a willing-seller, willing-buyer approach to land reform secured, thereby protecting minority interests for a ten-year period. Further, land pricing was contingent upon market values, effectively limiting the government's ability to acquire lands for redistribution to the country's rural poor.[72]

On the expiration of the Lancaster House Agreement, and frustrated with the slowness of the willing-seller, willing-buyer approach, the government moved towards a non-voluntary land acquisition programme. This was based on a state-determined land pricing mechanism, and was institutionalised into the Land Acquisition Act (1993).[73] But scarce resources hampered the state: human and financial in formulating and implementing sustained and systematic land redistribution.

Thus, against the backdrop of land hunger due to rising poverty juxtaposed with vast under-utilised tracts of land owned by white commercial farmers, tensions began to rise. In order to be seen to be doing something, thereby maintaining credibility, the state, in 1994, appointed a Land Tenure Commission (LTC),[74] to examine the appropriateness of each of Zimbabwe's land tenure systems for its different farming sectors: Communal Areas (CA), Resettlement Areas (RA), Small Scale Farming Areas (SSFA) and Large Scale Commercial Farming Areas (LSCFA). On completion of this exercise, yet another phase of land redistribution was announced, based on the implementations of the commission's recommendations.

Within this phase, partial compensation was promised, covering buildings

---

72 Thus, the Land Tenure Commissions Report (1995) indicates that in the first decade of independence, approximately 52,000 families were resettled. This was far short of the 162,000-family target. Approximately 4,300 whites still owned about 40% of the land. About one million families remained in communal areas, with overpopulation increasing annually.

73 Repealing the earlier Land Acquisition Act (1985), the 1993 Act enabled the government to: compulsorily acquire for public good, both under-utilised and used lands; pay a 'fair price' within a 'reasonable period' rather than paying promptly and at market-determined prices; and fix the compensation for land acquired through a committee of six persons through set valuation guidelines. Moyo, S. (1995). *The Land Question in Zimbabwe.* Harare: SAPES.

74 The Commission comprised agricultural specialists, lawyers, academics, and traditional chiefs, only one member of the LTC was a women. They undertook year-long consultations with key government ministries and civil society organisations. Public hearings were held at provincial, district, communal, village, resettlement, small- and large-scale commercial farming locations to gain evidence and make recommendations regarding land redistribution.

and infrastructure rather than land value. But while ZANU-PF continued to posture as if redistribution would go forward, the WB, the IMF, the British government, and other groups sided with white farmers and effectively vetoed any forced sales, throughout 1997 and 1998. Thus a donor conference held in 1998 sought support from the international community for land redistribution, which forced the government to concede that any land taken would be paid for up front.[75]

But while ZANU-PF was being pulled in one direction by foreign funder prerogatives, just as importantly there was pressure coming in another direction: from civil society.[76] From the mid-1980s civil society's disparate voice began to resist through campaigns against ESAP and regulation of civil society organisation through the Private and Voluntary Organisations Act (PVO). This paved the way to more sustained organising and coalition-building in the mid- to late 1990s around economic reform, debt, land, the constitution, human rights and democratic governance.

At the same time, the trade unions became more vocal. The Zimbabwe Congress of Trade Unions (ZCTU) called for a general strike 'that could paralyse the nation'.[77] Unexpected civil service militancy emerged, indicating the level of dissention within the state, and for nearly a fortnight in mid-1996, a strike of more than two-thirds of the civil service paralysed the government. Daily demonstrations in Harare showed that workers were ratcheting up the pressure on Robert Mugabe[78] and the state folded to demands. Following this example, 100,000 private sector workers were involved in strike action in mid-1997. Again real wage increases were finally won. As one paper put it: 'Never before in Zimbabwe's history have so many workers gone on strike demanding better salaries and improved working conditions then in the last few months ...'[79]

---

75 Noting that a total of Z$4million had been set aside for this exercise!
76 There is a wealth of diverse theorising, analysis and debate on the nature and function of civil society and in Zimbabwe. The terms civil society, and NGO are often used synonymously to imply a set of urban organisations/actors that engage with the state and direct civil society action. Following from this, NGOs in Zimbabwe – the most visible inhabitants of contemporary civil society – become slippery to define. Ranging from women's rights groupings, and the Catholic Church, to chambers of commerce, these organisations are often defined negatively in relation to the state, but may engage in pro-state activity. See Moyo, S., Makumbe, J. & Raftopoulos, B. (2000), who offer an abbreviated history of civil society in Zimbabwe, in which the role of women is largely passive.
77 160,000 workers. See the *Zimbabwe Independent*, August 1996, 'ZCTU Threatens General Strike'.
78 Who had just returned from his honeymoon, after marrying Grace Marufu.
79 *Financial Gazette*, 17 July 1997, 'Strikes Blow Lid Off Simmering Economic Pot'.

It was, however, a Catch-22 situation as workers were finding it impossible to live on current wages while companies were struggling to survive under market reform.

These victories meant that when the economic downspin began in late 1997,[80] the Zimbabwe Congress of Trade Unions (ZCTU) could easily step in to assume national oppositional leadership. Well-organised general strikes and demonstrations in December 1997 and March and November 1998 won nearly universal worker support. In high-density communities, days of rioting over food and petrol price hikes left several people dead at the hands of the police in both January and November 1998. Emblematic of the growing conflict, then trade unionist leader, Morgan Tsvangirai, was badly beaten by ZANU-PF supporters after the first successful national strike and a few months later the second most important ZCTU office, in Bulawayo, was burnt to the ground.

ZANU-PF leaders attempted to put out various fires within the party, as confidence in Mugabe's leadership plummeted, and the geographically and ethnically fragmented nature of the party required a strong-arm leader simply to serve as glue to give the appearance of preparedness for the upcoming 2000 parliamentary and 2001 presidential elections.

The declining economy made political crisis management all the more difficult. Reacting to the political challenges, Mugabe repeatedly overstretched, first through the gazetting of a regulation rendering strikes illegal. Then, in September 1998, without consultation, Mugabe sent thousands of army troops to the Democratic Republic of the Congo (DRC) in defence of Laurent Kabila, who was under attack by Rwandan- and Ugandan-backed rebels.[81] Mugabe's intervention was seen as a crucial, if temporary, crutch to Kabila's rule, particularly during 1998 when Kabila refused to meet the rebels for peace talks. The rationale for the intervention was widely understood to include the economic interests of the ruling party.

Amidst these events, there was other political noise rising in the background. In early 1999, the army illegally detained a journalist and the editor[82] of *The Standard,* a weekly newspaper that reported an alleged coup attempt, followed by the arrest of four other journalists on grounds of malicious reporting about the DRC war. This led to a confrontation between Mugabe and the highest level of the judiciary, with Mugabe resorting to race-baiting his opposition as agents

---

80 See above.
81 *Financial Gazette,* 10 September 1998, 'Mugabe Raises Stakes in DRC Crisis'.
82 Roy Choto and Mark Chanvunduka respectively.

of British imperialism.[83] Demands came from the indigenous business lobby, which claimed they were still shut out of 'white-controlled' markets and financial institutions. Early in 1998, university students took to the streets, as more general popular alienation from government intensified with each new revelation of political and civil service corruption.

With Zimbabwe at its most politicised level in two decades, the time was right for consolidated organised resistance. This came from within the ranks of civil society through the birth of the National Constitutional Assembly (NCA).[84] This coalition sought to build a broad alliance of civic organisations[85] around the issue of constitutional reform. Its central objective was to raise the level of national consciousness on the need for a new constitution, and a review of the Lancaster House Constitution,[86] and after consultation, draft a 'homegrown Zimbabwean Constitution' in a manner that evoked genuine national debate.

The NCA became the most vocal and major challenging factor to ZANU-PF by bringing the constitutional debate out onto the streets and to rural communities as early as 1998. Its impact on the political scene exceeded all expectations[87] as the NCA became the largest civil society coalition formed in the post-independence period. The coalition worked through an executive committee and task forces initially headed by Morgan Tsvangirai, the trade-union leader, a move that firmly cemented the alliance between the trade union movement and other civil society organisations.[88]

But in September 1999 Tsvangirai announced that the ZCTU had decided to establish a 'political formation' led by labour but with an enormous boost from allied progressive social forces, some of whom constituted the NCA. Thus the Movement for Democratic Change (MDC) was born and began to gain momentum. The political temperature was said to have 'shot up' as the MDC was seen as 'the biggest ever opposition party in Zimbabwe with the necessary national support'.[89]

---

83 Based on the judiciary's letter of rebuke after the army violated a court injunction to release the journalists.

84 Born in 1996.

85 Which was eventually to incorporate amongst others, the trade unions, students' movements, the mainstream churches, human rights organisations and media houses, women's groups and oppositional political parties.

86 Already amended sixteen times in 21 years. Notable amongst the amendments was the vesting of power in an omnipotent president in 1987.

87 As of September 2000, the NCA had over 30,000 registered individual members and 200 institutional members countrywide.

88 It became the home of leftist activists and the next generation of post-nationalist leaders.

89 *Financial Gazette*, 16 September 1999, 'MDC Launch Sets Stage for Bruising Battle'.

As constitutionalism came to the fore the state once again desperately needed to be seen to be doing something and so, in response, established the Constitutional Commission of Zimbabwe (CCZ).[90] It appointed approximately 400 commissioners to fulfil its main purposes of going out into villages, wards, districts and provinces gathering people's views on what they would like to see in a new constitution and drafting a new one. But from the outset this process was undemocratic and flawed and the content of the draft was not only 'contrary to what people said, but also not good for Zimbabwe'.[91]

The February 2000 constitutional referendum afforded the electorate a rare opportunity to register a vote of no confidence in Mugabe personally, and in the quality of government he was providing. The referendum was held with the aim of securing popular endorsement for an extravagant increase in presidential power, the strong rebuke came when a 'No' campaign gained 55% of the vote despite the full weight of the state machinery being thrown behind a 'Yes' vote. This decisive rejection suggested that, for the first time in the country's post-independence history, competitive elections were now possible and the ruling party was confronted with the possibility of defeat in the June 2000 parliamentary elections. It was during this period that the intensive data gathering phase of my research project was conducted.

The MDC, an infant opposition force, embodied the hope and vision for change not least of all with the slogan: 'Chinja, Maitero, Maitero Chinja,' 'Guqula Izenzo, Izenzo Guqula'.[92] But its subtle alignments and connections with the West were manipulated by the ZANU-PF regime to paint the MDC as a 'white' western-backed party. More importantly than this, the MDC's neo-liberal overtones presented some cause for caution.[93]

Be that as it may, the MDC was able to draw upon the enormous reservoir of hostility which by now had built up towards the Mugabe regime largely as a result

---

90 Established through an Act of Parliament the CCZ worked through an executive committee, and specific thematic, namely Customary Law and Practices, Executive Organs of the State, Separation of Powers, Levels of Government, Independent Commissions, Fundamental and Directive Rights, Public Finance and Management, Legal Committee, and Transitional Mechanisms committees and plenary forums.

91 2000. A Summary of the Main Features of the Draft CCZ Constitution: Some of the reasons why NCA campaigned for a 'no' vote. http://www.nca.org.zw/html/fdraft/fdraft_summ. htm See also, 'On The Constitutional Trail'. Zimbabwe Biz. November 1999. http://www. zimbabwebiz/magazine/11-1999/nov04.htm

92 In Shona and Ndebele respectively 'Now is the time, Fight for Change'.

93 As the Socialist Organisation has said there is more to politics than choosing between the devil and the deep blue sea.

of the endemic corruption of a ZANU-PF hierarchy, which was said to be en-riching itself at the expense of the population, and the blurring of lines between party and state, so that state property was manipulated, and even plundered at will. Virulence was further fuelled by the highly authoritarian political culture in which criticism of ZANU-PF, from whatever source, was considered treason-able, and the deep unpopularity of Mugabe's 1998 decision to deploy troops, by this stage 11,000 strong, at a cost of Z$30 million per month, in the seemingly futile regional conflict in the DRC. This military engagement was said to be ma-terially benefiting the ZANU-PF elite and the so-called 'businessmen-generals' as they gained access to that country's lucrative diamond sector and secured oth-er financial concessions from the beleaguered DRC regime of Laurent Kabila.

Tensions were further heightened as in 2000 inflation and interest rates stood at 70% and an estimated 50% of the workforce unemployed, coupled with rising poverty and chronic fuel shortages.

But, given that ZANU-PF had become an authoritarian force and given its determination to retain control over the state apparatus, a draconian response was inevitable in its post-referendum attempt to re-establish political hegemony. When the backlash came it was violent in character and involved a sustained attempt to intimidate by targeting MDC activists, candidates, and oppositional supporters for assault and abduction.[94]

The powerful evocation of nationalist struggle through the third chimurenga facilitated the unfolding of a race war with white farmers[95] being denounced by Mugabe as 'enemies of the state' and scapegoated for the country's problems. Mugabe began listing farms with a vow not to compensate farmers,[96] and the country plunged into violent land seizures. These illegal farm invasions were officially orchestrated, as ZANU-PF backed 'war veterans' moved onto 1,500 white-owned farms, with a partisan police force choosing to remain impassive in the face of murder and pillage and a xenophobic government attitude to all in-ternational criticism, particularly the British government in a transparent attempt

---

94 See Zimbabwe Human Rights NGO Forum: Reports on Political Violence. http://www.hrforumzim.com/frames/inside_frame_reps.htm

95 Less than 1% of the 12 million population.

96 In March 2000, section 16 of the constitution, which governs the private ownership of land, was amended. This stated that where the land was historically owned or occupied by indigenous people who were then dispossessed the obligation to pay compensation for the land rested with the British as former colonial power and not the Zimbabwean government. In April 2000, the constitution was again amended to enable the acquisition of commercial farms without obliging the government to pay for the land, but only the development on it.

by Mugabe to revive anti-colonial sentiment.

The land invasions, assaults and cases of intimidation prior to the 2000 parliamentary elections were reflective of long simmering tensions in this tumultuous national socio-economic and political context, except now they were sanctioned by the state. ZANU-PF recognised that the urban vote had largely been lost to the MDC, thus ZANU-PF's real target, was the rural peasantry, still comprising 65% of the population, whose votes would ultimately decide its fate. The ruling party sought to exploit the greater conservatism of rural communities, their deference to traditional structures, and the enthusiasm of the rural population for genuine land reform in a country where whites still owned two-thirds of the most fertile farming land.

Thus the farm invasions were designed to introduce the whole question of land ownership into the election campaign, primarily as a means of diverting attention from ZANU-PF's lamentable record in governance but also to coerce people, particularly in these rural communities, back into the party fold. Mugabe clearly believed that the issue of land reform was the trump card, which would secure his political salvation even if the means by which that goal was pursued entailed murder and wider social turmoil. This created a climate of fear in the country, a further erosion of Zimbabwe's already poor international image, the displacement of thousands, and the deaths of MDC supporters and members of the white farming community.

But while ZANU-PF officials had predicted throughout the parliamentary campaign period that the party would win a landslide victory, this was not the case. While in the lead-up to elections, MDC had to compete against a strong, pro-ZANU bias that was deeply entrenched within the political system; ZANU-PF enjoyed the support of a sycophantic official media that depicted the ruling party in heroic terms whilst routinely demonising the opposition. Moreover, the electoral register, for which the government had responsibility, was inaccurate and obsolete. It included the names of thousands of deceased and also the names of many others ineligible to vote, with some names being included more than once and in more than one constituency. The ruling party also kept a tight grip on the management of the election, restricting the number of foreign election monitors to a meagre 350 and delaying their formal accreditation, as well as hindering the access to polling stations of thousands of local monitors.

Yet, even in these most favourable of circumstances, ZANU-PF only scraped home against an opposition party barely nine months old, declining from 147 of the 150 seats to a likely 92, and from 117 of the elected seats to a mere 62. It was only those 30 nominated seats, to be distributed at the discretion of President Mugabe that gave ZANU-PF the illusion of a comfortable victory. The loaded parliamentary arithmetic meant that the MDC needed to win 76 of the elected seats to command a parliamentary majority as opposed to the 46, which would suffice for ZANU-PF.

Further, the MDC breakthrough was achieved in the face of 'brutality and intimidation' that destroyed all prospects of a 'free and fair election'.[97] Intimidation was most severe in rural constituencies, although most parts of the country were affected. Serious irregularities[98] throughout election campaigns and voting forced one to conclude that, 'the term free and fair elections is not applicable'.[99]

Thus the June 2000 elections should be seen as a hollow, even pyrrhic, victory for Robert Mugabe and ZANU-PF, although that seems unlikely given his apparent inability to detach his own personal interests, and those of the ZANU-PF hierarchy, from the wider interests of the nation. Instead, we are witnessing the latest re-enactment of a depressingly familiar post-colonial scenario that does not augur well for the possibility of a more democratic and accountable order; as I write Zimbabwe continues to slide into outright despotism and starvation.

---

97 The *Zimbabwe Independent*, 23 April 2000.
98 As described above.
99 The *Zimbabwe Independent*, 27 June 2000.

Chapter 4

ZIMBABWEAN WOMEN ORGANISING: 1980-1995

In this chapter I intend to give a history of the Zimbabwe women's movement from independence in 1980 through to 1995. In this way I hope to set the stage for an in-depth examination of the period under review and build a basis for further discussion and analysis.

There is little doubt that women's organising in Zimbabwe probably has a long and rich history. During pre-colonial times, gender relations must have undergone transformations. It is, however, in the work of Schmidt (1992),[100] that we first begin to find a gendered history. Not only does she challenge the way in which women are rendered invisible in conventional historiography, but she draws attention to the complex nature of gender relations in highlighting the impact of colonisation on women: one of the most detrimental aspects being the way in which indigenous systems of patriarchy colluded with strictures imposed by European men, who came from a world in which women had long been subjected to the authority of men.

With colonialism, significant numbers of African women are reported to have found refuge in mission compounds, where their 'saved souls' meant access to education. This missionary education, underpinned by European culture and ideas, has been aptly described as dedicated to the 'domestication' of African women, because of the manner in which it overlooked the multiple productive and reproductive roles of women, seeking instead to concentrate on homecrafts and housewifery. Some of the earliest documentation of women's organising in

---

100 In a study of Shona-speaking women in the period 1870-1939.

Zimbabwe is linked to this period.

Let's go back to the 70s or even the 50s. I don't think we can talk about a women's movement. There were women's organisations. I don't know if you can even call them women's organisations but there were these good wives kind of clubs that were teaching women to mend their husbands shirts, sew, cook and to make bread. Most of them were started by either white Zimbabweans ..., or by black women who used to go to church but who just didn't want to talk about anything else other than making women good wives. I didn't see it but I know it.[101]

Church organisations such as the Ruwadzano[102] of the United Methodist Church, is an example of one such club, but there were a variety aimed at making women become better wives and mothers. The Association of Women's Clubs (AWC)[103] was the first club that constituted itself as an organisation, to reach out to women in rural and urban communities.[104]

But as Schmidt observes, colonialism consolidated its hold, and European political institutions and practices extended their reach, while indigenous socio-political and economic systems, which appeared to have afforded women some status and influence amongst the Shona were gradually eroded and became dys-functional. In their place, a revamped version of 'customary law' was put to-gether reifying some of the most patriarchal aspects of indigenous cultures as they intersected with Victorian notions of womanhood. Codified customary law came to mediate relations between black men and women and under it a women remained a legal minor all her life, under the custodianship of her father, hus-band or eldest son.

African men grew accustomed to the extreme constraints placed on women, and the conservative majority did not espouse the notion that women were en-titled to rights of any kind. The immediate pre-independence period led to a reassessment of gender relations and this chapter of national history profoundly affected all aspects of social and political life, disrupting pre-existing gender rela-tions and cultural norms. The debates about gender roles came from two fronts: from women in the nationalist liberation movement, and from a small group of university-educated and professional women.[105]

With considerable numbers of women participating in the liberation struggle

101 Conversant transcript.
102 Established in 1919.
103 Established in 1938.
104 By 1958 there were five officially listed women's clubs, see Barnes and Win, op.cit. 1992.
105 Gaidzanwa, R. (1992).

in the late 1960s and 1970s, the image of the subservient mother or daughter came to be challenged by the female combatant.[106] Women proved to be just as able and dedicated to the cause for national liberation as their male counterparts and fuelled by socialist principles that underpinned the struggle, this left little justification for continued discrimination. Further, as opportunities to study abroad opened up, women made use of knowledge gathered from their own experiences in different educational institutions, societies and the international feminist movement, to develop critiques and to challenge gender subordination.

So, the move by the state in the first decade of independence to afford women superficial access to state structures and policies really arose out of a need to placate women. This was evident through the plethora of gender-sensitive legislative changes in the early 1980s. The Sex Disqualification Act (1980) allowed women to hold public office. New labour regulations[107] allowed equal pay for equal work and created the possibility for maternity leave. But it was the passing of The Legal Age of Majority Act (LAMA) in December 1982, affording all Zimbabweans legal status at the age of eighteen, which provoked outrage in traditional quarters as men accustomed to exercising full control over their daughters and wives suddenly found that they could no longer be assured of this. Under LAMA, women could now choose their sexual partners, inherit property, and engage in economic and political life.[108] LAMA was complemented by a series of laws that provided maintenance claims for women in unregistered customary marriages[109] and provision for the equitable distribution of matrimonial assets on divorce[110] making property grabbing by relatives of the deceased and dispossession of the surviving spouse and children, illegal.[111]

A Ministry for Community Development and Women's Affairs was established in 1981 and women who felt that the national structure would enable them to advance their interests, with the support of a government that was widely believed to be revolutionary,[112] enthusiastically welcomed this.

> *When the ministry of women started we were excited, one cannot talk about a movement without talking about the ministry, because it really helped, whether it*

---

106 Ibid. p. 110.

107 Minimum Wages 1980, Equal Pay Regulations 1980, Labour Relations Act 1984, Public Service Pensions (amendment) Regulations 1985.

108 At least in theory.

109 Customary Law and Primary Courts Act, 1981.

110 Matrimonial Causes Act No 33, 1985.

111 Deceased Person's Family Maintenance (amendment) Act, 1987.

112 The official philosophy of Marxist-Leninism was thought to be more progressive.

was conservative or otherwise, it helped in putting issues on the agenda.[113]

Welfare-orientated organisations like the AWC and Zimbabwe Women's Bureau (ZWB)[114] threw their weight behind the ministry and like many other civil society organisations were committed to national reconstruction and development. The ministry was never particularly powerful within government, but in its early days it did provide a valuable platform for the building of a gender consciousness and the exploration of feminist issues.

It was our training ground, some of us were created and are products of the ministry we got our strength from there … the women's meeting in Nairobi[115] *was key, there were a few women who went to Nairobi and when they returned they started looking at things differently. They came back with the Forward Looking Strategies*[116] *and started talking about patriarchy, about changing the status quo, we didn't know what they meant by changing the status quo…*[117]

This 'newly found' world view, where discrimination against women was as much about the personal as the political, resulted in frustration as women soon realised that the state was not interested in taking the necessary steps to overcome women's subordination in Zimbabwean society.

Women's access to paid employment, land and housing, issues of maintenance, and inheritance were not taken up by the Ministry and yet it was these issues that needed to be faced head on if women were to see any real change in their status.[118]

Women activists soon found themselves criticising the ministry's programmes which had been conceptualised within the women in development paradigm, seeking to add women on to mainstream development programmes without attending to the evidence that these were themselves part of the problem.[119] The ministry, in line with party dictates, limited its activities to supporting women within their highly circumscribed notions of their place in society. It consistently evaded any challenge to an oppressive and exploitative status quo. Thus the pro-

---

113 Conversant transcript.
114 Established in 1978.
115 The United Nations conference reviewing the 'women's decade' was held in Nairobi in 1985.
116 The Nairobi conference resulted in the 'Forward Looking Strategies for the Advancement of Women to the Year 2000' which was adopted by all participating governments and formed the yardstick by which countries assessed their progress in improving the conditions of women regionally, nationally and globally.
117 Conversant transcript.
118 Conversant transcript.
119 Little attention was paid to the growing body of evidence that 'development' has often upheld male interests to the detriment of women's.

grammes to which they were committed were reflective of an unreconstructed gender politics.

> *You see the ministry started where the churches left off … it went straight into projects, but I think what had changed was the fact that they were addressing income generation and a narrowly defined community development. There was no change in the status quo; there was nothing about addressing patriarchal structures. The ministry could only go so far and no further … anyway by 1988 it was reshuffled, changed and baptised a different name – the Ministry of Community Development, that was the end of it.[120]*

Operation Clean-Up

As these manifestations of power and patriarchy began to surface, a state of moral panic was developing across the nation, fuelled by endless media reports of schoolgirl pregnancies, prostitution, divorce, and baby dumping, all of which blamed women for moral decadence and attributed 'feminism' to undesirable 'foreign influences'.[121]

The contradictory nature of the official position was starkly illustrated in October 1983, when the authorities suddenly carried out large-scale raids all over the country, arbitrarily rounding up thousands of women, subjecting them to humiliation and abuse, and detaining them in subhuman conditions.

> *This assault was officially known as Operation Clean-Up and its purpose was to round up single women out alone and charge them with being prostitutes. The soldiers and police followed their instructions enthusiastically. Over 6,000 women were arrested, including old women, schoolgirls as young as 11 years old, young mothers with babies on their backs, nurses coming off duty, and thousands of other innocent women... The arrests were not confined to women on the streets. In some cases police and soldiers invaded public places such as the theatre in Gweru and dragged women out.[122]*

Operation Clean-Up was dramatic enough to provoke a change in Zimbabwean women's consciousness. It appeared that state patronage allowed little

120 Conversant transcript.
121 There are mixed views with regards women war veterans. Some women, who participated in the struggle, kept this quiet. The reason being that in some conservative circles, they were not considered heroines, or only briefly, but loose women. There were many tranditionalists and conservatives who felt women war veterans should not have left their homes, and were not liberators but 'prostitutes'. There was some ambivalence about their role, often unspoken, but extant for some years after independence.
122 Watson, P. (1998) *Determined to Act.* Harare: WAG, p. 7.

room for the advancement of women's rights and with this gradual recognition a different kind of women's organisation was born. The new activism took place outside the state and brought women from different sections of Zimbabwe's still divided society together around gender interests for the first time.

The Women's Action Group (WAG) began in 1983 when a small group of Harare-based women called a series of public meetings that brought women together to discuss the outrages perpetuated under Operation Clean-Up. The core group of 40-50 women engaged in advocacy work on behalf of women, acting as a pressure group and carrying out campaigns. On 5-6 May 1984 WAG organised a workshop on the theme 'Zimbabwean Women Speak Out'. Over 400 women from all walks of life attended. Rural women joined professional urban women. Farmers, factory workers, university teachers and nurses sat and discussed their problems, expressed their views and listed their recommendations.

This really changed things, many of us in the ministry were frustrated and moved out, then you got younger women who were coming out of university and who were enthusiastic. We were trying to understand what was meant by a women's movement, what women's organisations elsewhere were doing. In 1990 you saw the birth of many organisations...we were very active during this period, meeting, thinking and talking, we would meet at each others houses, to plan... there was energy and spaces were created for addressing women's concerns and issues.[123]

Increasing consciousness and the growing recognition of injustices perpetrated against women meant that WAG was soon joined by a plethora of organisations. The decade, 1985-95, initially at least, saw both black and white women working together to challenge the patriarchal precepts of a society that tolerated the abuse of women by men, and the increasing invocation of tradition to validate discriminatory behaviour. The Musasa Project was established in 1988 and set out to address the visible and growing issue of violence against women. National branches of Women and Law in Southern Africa – Research and Education Trust (WLSA) and Women in Law and Development in Africa (WiLDAF) were established in Harare in 1989 and 1990 respectively. The Federation of African Media Women Zimbabwe (FAMWZ, established 1985), focussed on women in the media, the Women and AIDS Support Network (WASN, established 1989), sought to deal with the growing HIV/AIDS pandemic, the Zimbabwe Women's Resource Centre and Network (ZWRCN, established 1990), focused on research and documentation, advocacy and the distribution of information

---

123 Conversant transcript.

on gender issues. The Zimbabwe Women's Finance Trust (ZWFT, established 1989) and Zimbabwean Women in Business (WIB, established 1995) concentrated on women's economic interests while the Zimbabwe Women Lawyers Association (ZWLA, established 1992) sought to assist poorer women with legal advice, while lobbying for legal reform in areas of the law that discriminate against women.

By 1995, there were over 25 registered women's organisations[124] independently addressing various aspects of women's lives in urban and rural areas. Some of these organisations worked in both urban and rural areas,[125] cultivating a substantial rural constituency. If one wants to categorise, I could say that these NGOs and CBOs spanned the range of practical and strategic gender interests working within the paradigms of women in development, women and development, and gender and development (WID, WAD and GAD). There existed a conceptual unevenness in understandings and articulations of gender as a political struggle. Thus, some of these organisations were overtly feminist in orientation, others more conservative and mainstream in their approaches. Nonetheless, in the 1990s, they all played a role in re-defining the private and public sphere, demanding full rights for women as citizens of the state.

Despite initial atomisation, by the mid-1990s these organisations came to constitute a loose network as each developed an operational niche or sector, complementing the work of sister organisations in formal and informal arrangements in the struggle for gender justice.

Strictures on Non-State Organising

In the early 1990s, the AWC, the longest standing women's organisation, began to re-invigorate itself, accumulating over 40,000 largely rural members, and pledges of over eleven million Zimbabwe dollars for programmes scheduled to run between 1994 and 1998. However, these achievements were rapidly curtailed when the AWC became the first, and to date only, NGO to be suspended under what was known as the Private Voluntary Organisations (PVO) Act.

> *The PVO Act, passed into the laws of Zimbabwe in 1995 and was a substantive departure from its predecessor,[126] in respect of the extensive powers given to the Minister of Public Service, Labour and Social Welfare to dismiss officials of vol-*

---

124 FOS Directory..
125 Notably the Association of Women's Clubs, Zimbabwe Women's Bureau, Women's Action Group, Zimbabwe Women's Resource Centre and Network, Jekesa Pfungwa.
126 The Welfare Organisations Act.

untary organisations without being required to lay formal charges, while permitting the state to search, seize and dispose of its property.[127] The implications of the Act were brought home through the gazetting of the AWC on 2 November 1995. The one-page Government Gazette announced the suspension of the Executive Committee, except for two members from the Mashonaland region and and replaced them with women deemed to be 'loyal' to the ZANU-PF's Women's League[128]

With frozen funds and no organisational base, the AWC executive under the Chairpersonship of Sekai Holland,[129] took on and fought the state for the right to exist autonomously, and to organise and mobilise women to achieve their own empowerment. The gazetted women, took their case to the Supreme Court in May of 1996 challenging the legality of the section under whose terms they had been charged: denial of a fair hearing, and freedom of expression, abuse of the right to freedom of association and assembly. In early 1997 the Supreme Court[130] ruled unanimously in favour of the women.[131]

Up until this point, the state had a fairly broad basis of legitimacy founded on the legacy of the liberation struggle and its development goals. As such, its rule was characterised by popular consent, however conditional and uneven. Civil society sought to avoid a frontal confrontation with the state through a complex mix of strategic positioning and carefully selected political vocabulary; the priority was to maintain a viable relation with government in pursuance of a complementary developmentalist agenda. But against the backdrop of increasing fragmentation through ESAP, increasing corruption and increasing fragmentation within civil society,[132] civics began to grow increasingly vocal in their criticism

---

127 In contradiction with section 11 and 17 of the Zimbabwean constitution which protects privacy of property and property from arbitrary search and seizure respectively.

128 While the scope of this study limits a more in-depth exploration of party political manifestations of women's organising, ZANU-PF Women's League, the women's wing of the ruling political party, has been a contentious space in reproducing the policies of the state and reinforcing women's traditional subservient roles. In 1994 ZWRCN observed that the presence of singing, dancing and kneeling of Women's League members at the Harare International Airport when dignitaries arrive, had become a well-known but controversial aspect of women's affairs. The *Daily Gazette* of 12 July 1994 wrote: '*If government is seriously interested in abolishing the traditional inequality of women, it should stop the humiliating spectacle of party women kneeling before the head of state at airport ceremonies, while men remain standing.*'

129 At one stage a ZANU stalwart.

130 At this stage, 1997, still autonomous and independent.

131 To date no report on the conclusions of these investigations has been made public and no evidence to substantiate the allegations has been given.

132 It is important to note that with increasing economic precariousness and donor aid, civil society became a site of accumulation for the middle class and some individuals and

of the state's failure to deliver social and economic security and good governance. Increasingly this oppositional stance infuriated a state whose credibility was being called into question. The PVO Act was just one attempt at legislative control. But in the mid-1990s, civil society was also somewhat uncoordinated, and despite efforts to challenge the PVO Act,[133] there was limited impact in overthrowing the legislation.

While the PVO became a vehicle for a very clear message to broader civil society in the face of its growing criticism of the state, little attention was given to the fact that the PVO act was employed on one of the oldest women's organisations in Zimbabwe.

Some women's organisations pooled their energies with other civic groups to challenge the PVO. But this meek effort displayed a lack of capacity to defend another NGO and band together for sustained collective action.

The state's mixed messages regarding its gender politics may be one of the factors that can lead to our understanding of the apparent lack of militancy regarding the PVO Act. Up until this point the state exhibited a tendency to grant rights to women, retracting them at will through the use of force if necessary. If we look briefly at the development, or in this case retraction, of the national machinery, it highlights the same trend.

National Machinery

As I noted above, in 1988 the Ministry of Women's Affairs was subsumed by community development and co-operatives. Subsequently, with ZANU-PF domination, it was further weakened following a merger with the Ministry of Political Affairs that downgraded women's affairs to a department within the ministry. Here it lost any semblance of autonomy, becoming marginalised within the state bureaucracy.

In 1993 it was relocated again, this time into the Ministry of National Affairs, Employment Creation and Co-operatives (MNAECC), under male management but supported by Deputy Minister Shuvai Mahofa. It was reduced to a 'women and development unit' with only three staff. Its mandate was to:

Advance the status of women at all levels in all sectors; to mainstream gender into

---

institutions were benefitting from aligning themselves to the state deliberately or through co-option. In this way, the state also contributed to the weakening of civil society.

133 Civil Society initiated the PVO Act Campaign Group led by: Zimbabwe Project, Streets Ahead, Housing People of Zimbabwe, Ecumenical Support Services, ZimRights and Mwengo.

all national programmes, policies and projects; to monitor national and international commitments; to mobilise Zimbabwe on important occasions like international women's day.[134]

The unit was also to liase with other government ministries involved in promoting the advancement of women and safeguarding their rights through the establishment of Gender Focal Points (GFP). But, needless to say, staffing inadequacies, structural constraints and gross under-funding coupled with a conservative patriarchal leadership,[135] which informed the ruling party line severely curtailed any meaningful progress.[136]

In 1998 the state further confused its gender agenda by creating a Minister of Gender appointed as a Minister of State in the President's office. The Minister of Gender, Oppah Muchinguri, was responsible for monitoring the mainstreaming of gender in all government ministries; in effect evaluating the role of the women's unit in MNAECC. While some saw this as an indication of the importance of gender on the national agenda, it could also be read as a sign of proliferating the bureaucracy and obfuscating the playing field. Predictably, lines of communication and responsibility became blurred and power struggles ensued.

Oppah Muchinguri, the first minister, had the insight to realise the importance of working with women's organisations. Sustained efforts at capacity building and information provision were undertaken via the network Working Group on Gender Politics (WGGP). In order to inform debate, this group provided female MPs with analysis on the gender implications of bills discussed in parliament. But, while sometimes effective,[137] generally such consciousness-raising activities were often frustrated by party politics.

By the mid-1990s women's organisations saw the need to consolidate and work together in confronting an increasingly hostile state that found itself under immense pressure from various sectors. The failed resettlement programme[138]

---

134 ZWRCN (2000). 'The National Machinery for Women in Zimbabwe: An NGO Assessment'. Accra: *Third World Network*, p. 4.

135 Within which some women members of parliament were beneficiaries and well rewarded advocates.

136 Ibid. p. 31.

137 It was through this process of linking with women MPs that the Administration of Estates Bill was stayed and reviewed.

138 Failure on three counts: to develop a meaningful land reform programme; to support those programmes where land was redistributed e.g. through the co-operatives, or through nationalisation; to consider the importance of secondary industries arising out of the agricultural sector.

placed enormous pressure on the government to deliver in terms of land reform, the tenets of the struggle for liberation. This meant that white farmers and black empowerment groups were both vying for the ear of the state in trying to protect their own interests. The IMF and World Bank too were beginning to dictate economic policy in the light of a failing economy and the majority of Zimbabwean people were beginning to feel the increasing pinch of structural adjustment.

While women's organisations had begun to come together to discuss and debate in the past, the first forays into sustained collective action came through the lobbying and advocacy around women's rights and access to land followed by constitutional reform and electioneering. The following chapter therefore details the mobilisation of the Zimbabwe women's movement in these areas in the period 1995-2000.

Chapter 5

LAND, LAWS AND VOTES FOR WOMEN

Women constitute over 70% of the people living in rural areas. As such the issue of land is one that touches their survival and livelihood to the core. Since the early years of independence, problems of women's access to and control over land and other productive agricultural resources has been raised at most fora and in almost all studies on gender. It still remains the most contested and unresolved problem. The unwillingness by government to fundamentally change the status quo has been seen by many activists as one of the key indicators of the state's unwillingness to alter the balance of power for the benefit of the majority of women. Even within the current debates and political manoeuvres on land redistribution, the concerns of women have been ignored and, on more than one occasion, the top leadership has indicated that gender issues are not on the list of priorities.[139]

By the mid-1990s it was clear that gender concerns were incidental in the mindset of the Zimbabwean government. While the lethargy of land redistribution remained a thorn in the side of the nation, for women the dream of having access to and control over land and allied resources was rapidly evaporating, as traditional forms of social organisation and values were implicated in complex ways in the ideology and practice underpinning land redistribution.

Land rights in traditional communities were conferred upon marriage to a family unit and not to individuals, thus land was guaranteed to every adult sufficient for their needs. Women's rights to land were particularly protected through the *tseu* or *isivande* practice,[140] but distortion of the interpretation of African cus-

---

139 Conversant transcript.
140 In which women were allocated their own piece of land.

43

tom and practice through colonisation has eroded these practices with negative consequences for women, as minors under the perpetual protection of a male, women are limited to secondary land-use rights as supported by my research:

> *We went to Mashonaland West, Matabeleland and Masvingo, we just wanted to find out whether women have access to land. That's when I discovered … women are not accessing land because traditional leaders sometimes refuse to register them. They send women away and sometimes they are told that the man must be the one to come and register. If she's a widow or a women who has been deserted by her husband then she has a problem in actually having her name registered … I want to see whether women have been registered and if they are registered do they actually get land and if they don't what were the reasons.*[141]

With the appointment of the LTC[142] in 1993, the ZWRCN and Rudecon Zimbabwe co-ordinated initial consultative programmes with women farmers[143] in order to gain evidence and make substantive submissions to the Commission. The report[144] submitted to the LTC clearly articulated women's experiences and demands with regards land tenure making specific recommendations in relation to the particularities of access in each sector and more generally calling for:

> *Land rights to be afforded regardless of their marital status, government to establish a quota system for women who needed land in all sectors, gender representation at all levels of decision-making to ensure gender sensitivity, the redefinition of 'heads of households' to mean both spouses, leases to be registered in the name of both spouses where the applicant is married.*[145]

After the submissions, extensive research, along with numerous public discussions in urban and rural areas, continued. These were directed at continuing to assess and monitor the gender dimensions of land distribution through the lived experiences of women farmers. NGOs working in this area[146] organised meetings with commissioners and government officials in order to raise awareness and lobby to gain support for a gendered perspective on land reform.

---

141 Conversant transcript.

142 The Land Tenure Commission was established by President Robert Mugabe, to examine the appropriateness of each of Zimbabwe's land tenure systems, see Chapter 3.

143 Organising focused on women's access to and control of land in Communal and Resettlement areas. Women were further disadvantaged with respect to SSCFA and LSCFA where access remained skewed on the basis of race and class.

144 See ZWRCN (1994). *The Gender Dimension of Access and Land Use Rights in Zimbabwe: evidence to the Land Commission.* Harare: ZWRCN.

145 WLLG.

146 At this stage ZWRCN and Rudecon Zimbabwe.

Organisations sought to lobby for land quotas for women and joint registration of spouses. The concentration was on resettlement areas where it felt there was a more realistic opportunity of getting greater gender equity because attitudes were less rigid, and local institutions were primarily those set in place by the state. Thus, this focus may have been strategic: resettlement areas are those where customary law is not yet established and so, in effect, more amenable to change.[147]

> *But historically, land was an issue that had evoked mobilisation along racial lines and re-focussing the struggle in terms of a gendered identity was irreconcilable, because it meant overthrowing the deep-seated understandings of custom and culture.[148]*

This became evident initially through the stance taken by the LTC with regard to gender issues. The Commission argued that it had no specific brief to look at the gendered dimension to land and the report that followed, while noting the gender inequalities inherent in land tenure,[149] stopped short of recommendations on equality mechanisms. This was all the more significant as its recommendations were to form the basis of subsequent governmental actions.

As national dialogue continued through the second phase of land redistribution, women became increasingly vociferous in their articulations and consolidated their efforts through the formation of a land network called the Women and Land Lobby Group (WLLG).[150] This group pooled its skills and organisational credibility and was tasked on behalf of its constituency to direct and steer all lobbying, advocacy and civic education efforts in relation to land rights. The WLLG sustained advocacy efforts, forming alliances with civil society organisations as a means of furthering the gender agenda, maintaining consultative dialogue with women farmers and negotiations with the state in a climate that saw the issue of land becoming increasingly contested and politicised.

---

147 It should, however, be noted that the emphasis on resettlement areas seems to lead to lack of understanding of communal areas. Arguing for corporate title in the form of clan rights, but with little recognition of whether this will leave women at the mercy of male systems regarding allocation and control.

148 Conversant transcript.

149 On the basis of the movement's reports. It highlighted the problematic nature of inheritance: the practice of the eldest son being appointed heir to his father's estate, including land, led to disputes between widows and brothers-in-law and between widows and minor children versus elder sons, but again the commission stopped short of recommending fundamental changes in favour of women. Inheritance was still still to be dealt with under the Administration of Estates Act.

150 The group was spearheaded by WAG, ZWRCN, Rudeçon Zimbabwe, Zimbabwe Farm Workers Trust, as well as concerned individuals.

But 'land was a no go zone and progress was elusive'.[151]

In September 1998 as the state sought support for a five-year programme of land reform from the international community,[152] this led them to seek pragmatic alliances with donors. The WLLG reading of the situation:

> *Money = power = ability to determine agendas. So we began to systematically lobby and form alliances with donors. We saw them as the channel to introduce gender as a conditionality for the state to access the much needed funds for a land redistribution programme.[153]*

In an attempt to produce a counter-narrative to the state's divisive evocation of an urban/rural split amongst women, the WLLG called on its cultivated organisational-member networks of women farmers and hosted a parallel conference in an adjacent room to the round-table donor meeting. Women farmers were therefore a visible presence, discussing the implications of existing land tenure systems and reiterating demands, which were taken to the plenary of the donor conference through donor alliances. 'We were riding high, the strategy was perfect, I remember everything came together, we thought we had achieved.'[154]

Indeed, women seemed to have won. The donor conditionality required government to include a gender component within land redistribution. But as had happened on previous occasions, gains were watered down and the state's hostility increased. The gender component of land reform lost its edge through the manipulation of gendered discourse. When the Minister of Agriculture was confronted with the question of women's participation and access to land and reform processes he:

> *Consistently denied to accept the need for special mechanisms instead adopted a gender neutral stance arguing that anyone can submit an application for consideration by the land re-distribution board, that in this respect women were not discriminated against. But we had the evidence that the procedures and regulations were inherently biased in favour of men.[155]*

Following the promise of resettlement land for ex-combatants, the WLLG began campaigning for one-third of designated land to be allocated to women in their own right, either individually or jointly with husbands. This demand was

---

151 Conversant transcript.
152 Estimated at US$1.5 billion, the President argued that without such assistance, the now sporadic land squatting phenomenon would turn into anarchy.
153 Conversant transcript.
154 Conversant transcript.
155 Conversant transcript.

not met. The WLLG then pushed for a 20% quota for women and continued lobbying for different forms of allocation and with regard to the concept of the family. But the minister was clear that joint ownership would not be enforced, arguing that this was a private matter, and that it was up to couples to decide in whose name the land was deemed to belong.[156]

More generally, women called for more transparency and participation in land policy formulation, for a rethinking of customary law in the constitution, for the need for clarifications on gender issues in law, and for a rethinking of the family and household as concepts.[157]

Predictably, the state saw 'its women' as colluding with the agents of 'western imperialism' in challenging 'traditional patterns' of land ownership. This hostility was to manifest most vehemently through the 1999 Magaya vs Magaya inheritance dispute.

But as Chapter 3 testifies, land was the ticket on which the ZANU-PF government would secure a fourth term of office. In late 1999, through the powerful evocation of a third *chimurenga*, the state snubbed the international community, began listing farms with a vow not to compensate mostly white commercial farmers. The country was plunged into confusion in the face of violent land seizures and occupations by 'war veterans'. How did this translate within the WLLG? Disjunction. Under nationalist discourses, the now institutionalised WLLG[158] came out in support of land invasions, which often used women as pawns in the process. Yet this stance was at odds with the organisations that formed its membership base.

Emerging differences in political vision and strategy led the founding organisations to problematise the institutionalising of a WLLG that was by this time entirely in charge of the land advocacy programme. Many of the WLLG's constituent members argued that:

> *Fast track is a temporary arrangement. If I go grab land, there are no laws to protect me. When fast track settles, women will be the first to lose the land. If we have not sorted out the things that stop women controlling land then the problems are still there.[159]*

In other words many took the position that land grabbing would undercut

---

156 WLLG (2001) p. 9.
157 WLLG (2001) p. 37/38.
158 The WLLG constituted itself as an NGO in mid-1999, as its constituent parts were under pressure and could not sustain the multiple and rigorous demands being placed upon them.
159 Conversant transcript.

the call for legal reform and the enshrining of women's rights.

Coalition Advocacy

During the years 1995-1998, women's organisations refined the strategy of co-ordinated coalition-building and action through numerous campaigns. It was a strategy that saw the organisational base, its rural networks and concerned individuals coming together in various configurations depending on the issues, disbanding and forming again in yet another constellation. Premature attempts in 1997 to consolidate this strategy through a co-ordinating body called the Women's Federation failed, but despite this, a high level of activism was sustained through numerous campaigns. Women organised and drew energy from international events and campaigns like the '16 days against gender-based violence', CEDAW reporting and the fourth World Conference on Women, held in Beijing.

Locally the aims embodied in the Beijing Platform for Action and CEDAW were translated through organisational projects and programmes. Women were vociferous in numerous advocacy efforts including the challenge to Constitutional amendment 14.

In 1995, The Supreme Court ruled[160] that a female citizen of Zimbabwe married to a 'foreigner' was entitled to reside permanently with her spouse in Zimbabwe, by virtue of the protection of freedom of movement under section 22(1) of the Constitution of Zimbabwe. This decision was historic in the sense that prior to this Supreme Court judgment, while men could confer automatic residence and citizenship upon their foreign wives, foreign husbands were subject to the discretionary powers of the department of immigration.

In doing this the Supreme Court once again acknowledged section 11 of the Constitution of Zimbabwe as a substantive section of the constitution. This was significant primarily because section 11 states in part that:

> *Whereas every person in Zimbabwe is entitled to the fundamental rights and freedoms of the individual, that is to say, the right whatever his race, tribe, place of origin, political opinions, colour, creed, or sex ...*

Women regarded this decision as a positive move towards greater gender equality. But in some government circles, including the presidency, the Supreme Court ruling was viewed as a direct challenge to governmental sovereignty and authority giving women a *carte blanche* to 'import' men of all persuasions into

---

160 Rattigan and Others v. the Chief Immigration Officer, Zimbabwe and Others. (Supreme Court of Zimbabwe, 1995).

Zimbabwe through the evocation of traditional and culturalist discourses. Thus once again the rights of women became contested terrain.

In December 1995, the government proposed the 14th Constitutional Amendment Bill. This amendment sought, amongst other things, to overturn the Supreme Court judgement by amending section 22 of the Constitution of Zimbabwe, once again restricting the rights of foreign husbands married to Zimbabwean women. There were several reasons for concern as one conversant has pointed out:

> *The bill was blatantly discriminatory. By legislating for a constitutional double standard with respect to marriage and citizenship, the bill was viewed as a direct attack on the gains Zimbabwean women had made since independence. The bill was also a direct infringement on the obligations of CEDAW.*[161]

Within a very short period a strategic alliance of various actors was formed[162] who engaged in advocacy efforts. This rapid action took place in the face of a speech[163] delivered by President Mugabe in which he acknowledged that women were 'up in arms' over the question of double standards, and in which he stated in no uncertain terms that in 'our culture' women must follow their husbands. Already, as early as 1996, there was a fear that all progressive steps would be lost; women, especially women parliamentarians, were in a tenuous position,[164] and there was fear that the general public would frightened to speak out against an issue when the president had stated his own views so clearly.

The group continued its advocacy efforts strategising and re-strategising. They lobbied government ministers, including the Minister of Justice Legal and Parliamentary Affairs, Emmerson Mnangagwa, and the Minister of Home Affairs, Dumiso Dabengwa, while pushing for an audience with the President. In March 1996 the Minister of Justice announced that:

> *...As a result of the debate, Cabinet reconsidered the Bill at its meeting of 5th*

---

161 Zimbabwe was a signatory of CEDAW, which it ratified in 1991.

162 Included representatives of WiLDAF, Zimbabwe Lawyers for Human Rights, Men's Forum on Gender (PADARE), ZIMRIGHTS, ZWRCN, Women's Action Group (WAG), ZWLA, Zimbabwe Council of Churches (ZCC), Catholic Commission for Justice and Peace and the Legal Resources Foundation (LRF).

163 Mugabe's annual pre-birthday interview in which he was able to gain electoral ground by raising issues pertinent to his campaign.

164 Women parliamentarians were tenuously positioned as they had to toe the party line and many were in positions as a result of long and complex lines of patronage. This is compounded by the fact that just because you are a women does not mean you are committed to a transformatory political agenda, something that raises questions for quotas in parliament.

March and decided to adopt a gender-neutral approach to questions of citizenship and residence. The Bill will be amended to provide that every foreigner, regardless of gender or marital status, will be subject to the same screening process before he or she is accepted for residence in Zimbabwe.[165]

This development was disturbing. Instead of using the opportunity to enhance human rights, the government had effectively chosen to make discrimination gender neutral, thereby removing a constitutionally held provision. As one conversant put it:

[O]ur efforts outlawed gender as a basis for discrimination. It put male and female spouses of Zimbabwean citizens on a similar basis in terms of right of entry into Zimbabwe based on marital relationship. But as it turned out it became a form of negative equality.

Many more radical forms of activism also took place during this period and there are a number of examples that can be cited as testimony to this. Spaces were opened for debate on *lobola*[166] and marriage. The Working Group on Gender Politics (WGGP) sought to capacitate and build alliances with women MPs through discussion, and the provision of rigorous gendered analyses of forthcoming parliamentary bills. In this way, the WGGP worked with women parliamentarians, who in 1996 staged a walk out and by doing this ushered in the victory of the Administration of Estates Act in the same year, a landmark amendment that provided for the rights of surviving spouse/s in an intestate estate.

The movement supported the installation of the first woman chief, Sinqobili Mabhena, in Matabeleland early in 1997. Later in that year, the Oma[167] bank was mooted. The idea was first put forward by the Ministry of Community Development and Women's Affairs and was seen as a means by which rural women could access credit. Although the idea received resounding support, it did not take off the ground.

The movement initiated vociferous protests against rising sexual harassment and violence against women,[168] and the stripping of young women wearing miniskirts and tight-fitting trousers by men who argued that *they* prefer 'traditional

---

165 Press Release 7 March 1996 'Constitution of Zimbabwe Amendment (No 14) Bill' (inserted by Hon. E. D. Mnangagwa, Minister of Justice, Legal and Parliamentary Affairs).

166 Bride price.

167 Oma standing for *omana/madzimai* – women only.

168 Which often involved government officials as in April 1998 male MP, Solomon Mujuru, a former army chief and a hero of Zimbabwe's war of independence had to be restrained from assaulting an outspoken independent female MP Margaret Dongo.

dress'.[169] However this flurry of activity did not necessarily lead to meaningful transformation of gender relations in Zimbabwe. In fact, meaningful progress was somewhat illusory and circumscribed. It was the Magaya[170] ruling of the Supreme Court of Zimbabwe that proved this. In illustrating how gains can be abrogated, 'it brought centre stage the interface and tensions between customary and general law, culture, tradition and women's rights'.[171]

One Step Forward Two Steps Back

In 1999 Venia Magaya became a symbol of resistance to the negative interpretations of customary law in Zimbabwe when the Supreme Court ruled that LAMA does not provide for women to be treated as adults under customary law. Through its ruling in the inheritance case, Magaya vs Magaya, the court overruled prior cases confirming women's rights to inherit under customary law.[172] It indicated that cases allowing women to sue in their own right had, in fact, been wrongly decided. Thus the Court underscored the injustices suffered by women under customary law, stating that the inequities were justified by the patriarchal nature of the society and the necessity of maintaining a patrilineal tradition.

The facts of the case are fairly simple, but the Court's argument supporting the decision is convoluted. Venia Magaya was the only child of her father's first marriage. She had three half-brothers from his second marriage. When the father died intestate, Venia Magaya claimed status as heir and was appointed such by the community court. Her half-brother objected on grounds that not all the family had been notified of the proceedings. Venia's inheritance was cancelled, and her half-brother was granted status as heir under customary law, as the oldest claiming male child. He proceeded to evict Venia from her house. Upon challenge, the Supreme Court held that as to intestate succession, the custom of male preference for heirship, even when there is senior female offspring, must be applied. In so holding, the Court overruled all prior rulings in which LAMA had been applied.

In a circular argument, the Court stated that the discrimination suffered by women under customary law is not a matter of perpetual minority but is a result of the:

> *[n]ature of African society, especially the patrilineal, matrilineal, or bilateral na-*

---

169 Which women's organisations argued was a loincloth or nothing at all!
170 Magaya vs Magaya SC 210/98.
171 Conversant transcript.
172 The Administration of Estates Act 1997.

> *ture of some of them... allowing female children to inherit... would disrupt the*
> *African customary laws of that society... I am also of the view that the finding*
> *[in cases applying LAMA to provide inheritance and other rights to women] is*
> *tantamount to bestowing on women rights they never had under customary law.*[173]

That, of course, is precisely the point. LAMA did give women rights they had not had under customary law.

> *It gives them the right to be treated as adults and to challenge men on an equal legal*
> *footing. What the Court really says in this opinion is that women are adult persons*
> *for some purposes in Zimbabwean society, regardless of custom, but not for others,*
> *where male power over property and over women's fate is threatened.*[174]

Against the backdrop of international outcry and national debate on a new constitution[175] women activists took to the streets, delivering a protest to the Supreme Court; supportive MPs, lawyers and women activists strategised on how to enshrine watertight provisions for gender equality. The ruling was a clear indication of the need for constitutional reform as Zimbabwe's constitution is, in the words of then law lecturer Welshman Ncube, 'decidedly undecided on gender equality'. Zimbabwe's constitution allows for customary law to

> *sneak in by affirming the nature of African society even when it discriminates*
> *against women or goes against international conventions signed by Zimbabwe. Cus-*
> *tomary law expresses the values of a patriarchal, agrarian society. General law*
> *has gradually incorporated principles of gender equality as the nation evolved.*
> *Independence did not solve this dichotomy. Both systems coexist, uncomfortably.*[176]

Further, although convenient for authorities, the reduction of customary law into written form 'ossifies a system which is essentially evolutionary and does not allow it to evolve to meet modern socio-economic circumstances' concludes a study on inheritance practices in six southern African countries by Women and Law in Southern Africa[177].

But while some women activists wanted to maintain a modified version of customary law as the root of African culture and tradition, a feminist analysis saw customary law as a patriarchal convention, codified during the colonial era to control women's productive and reproductive capacities. Thus the feminists took

---

173 Original ruling, p. 15.
174 Conversant transcript.
175 See below.
176 Conversant transcript.
177 WLSA 1993. Inheritance Laws and Practices. WLSA: Harare.

the debate one step further, saying, in effect: 'chuck it out!'[178]

Customary law must go because it excludes women. Africa trades with the world using modern laws. Why can't these apply to African women? Africa cannot go into the next millennium carrying this unchuit baggage.[179]

Noting that views were diverging and that this heterogeneity was not being given the time or space to be discussed within the movement, women activists turned to the constitutional review process as the ultimate forum for enshrining gender equality and entrenching Zimbabwean women's rights.

Constitutional Reform

The recognition and realisation of the power of collective organising was re-alised through women's participation in the constitutional reform process. The women's network quickly realised that in order to make an impact in a national debate where women's voices stood a good chance of being marginalised they needed to protect their own interests. More so, because at its inception[180] the National Constitutional Assembly (NCA), the space created by the 'left' within civil society in Zimbabwe, was male-dominated with three women participating at its inception.

I entered the constitutional debate through the NCA and I will tell you that it was male centred. The debate was male; the faces that were fronting the debate were male, the issues raised were male issues... We realised we were in trouble, because every time we tried to raise anything at the task force, we had to sit strategically next to sympathetic men and ask these guys to paraphrase, because if you tried to speak as a woman, it was not taken on.[181]

The government-initiated Constitutional Commission of Zimbabwe (CCZ) on the other hand was not without its problems in relation to transparency and accountability:

ZANU-PF claimed to be the mouthpiece of the society; the initiation of any changes; the representatives of the interests of the povo; and indeed the crucible of all knowledge about what the society wanted. It was therefore the prerogative of ZANU-PF to decide what the new constitution would look like ... that's before the consultations even began.[182]

---

178 Conversant transcript.
179 Conversant transcript.
180 Period 1996 to mid-1998.
181 Conversant transcript..
182 Conversant transcript.

Given the government's track-record the CCZ's receptiveness to gender issues was questionable. When the CCZ was established it had 52 women, 13% of its total representation. Some of the women invited to serve as commissioners were active within the women's movement.[183] As expected, despite an outcry from various quarters regarding women's low representation on the commission, given the importance of the task at hand, no redress was forthcoming.

Thus with two parallel processes underway and neither space ideal for women to explore their own concerns and consolidate demands, women's organisations came together to form the Women's Coalition on the constitution. This action was informed by their years of experience of coalition advocacy and an analysis that led them to place much weight on the constitutional process. 'Most of the problems that women face with regards to gender discrimination, with particular reference to customary law or culture, have their roots in the Constitution'.[184] And, constitutional reform created an opportunity for women to deal with the supposed 'root causes'.

The coalition comprised a network of over 60 women activists, researchers, academics and representatives from 30 women's and other human rights organisations.[185] Launching itself in June 1999, the Women's Coalition aimed to:

> *Unite women around the constitution, provide information to women on the constitution reform process and gender issues therein which would constitute a critical mass for lobby and advocacy to engender the constitutional-making process and ensure the adoption of a constitution which protects women's political, social, economic and cultural rights.[186]*

With the understanding that:

> *The coalition will be inclusive, consisting of women of all possible races, linguistic and ethnic groups, classes, religions, occupations (including students), political parties, geographical locations, marital status and disabilities.[187]*

---

183 Notable amongst these were executive committee members and heads of the various thematic committees, Amy Tsango, Rita Makarau, Rudo Gaidzanwa, Lupi Mushayakarara, and Joyce Kazembe.

184 Conversant transcript

185 Member organisations included: AWC, Dorothy Duncan Centre for the Blind, Family Support Trust, FAMWZ, Harare Legal Projects Centre, Jekesa Pfungwa, Musasa Project, Mwengo, NCA, SAFAIDS, SAPES Trust, UZ-Law Faculty, WILDAF, WASN, WLSA, WLLG, Women, Leadership and Governance Institute, WAG, Working Group on Gender Politics, Young Women's Christian Association, ZAUW Residents Association, Zimbabwe Association of University Women, ZCC, ZWLA, ZWW, ZWB, ZWRCN.

186 Conversant transcript.

187 Minutes of the meeting of the Women's Coalition for the Constitution, 7 June 1999.

The coalition was organised through a management structure,[188] sub-committees and general membership. The task at hand was mammoth and from the outset members once again pooled resources and complemented each other's strengths and weaknesses in order to sustain a process that was not strictly bound by time and that did not necessarily fall within their organisational programming. What rapidly became evident was that:

> *At the time of the formation of the coalition there was so much energy amongst members, the togetherness was important and increasingly we started feeling comfortable just meeting as women … we needed our own space, we needed to define a women's agenda and stick to it to ensure that a gender dimension was integrated into a new constitution.*[189]

These goals were fulfilled through rigorous programming, which included a series of national and provincial consultative workshops and conferences to formulate a women's agenda. These consultations were held in both rural and urban areas. The coalition also embarked on an aggressive media campaign on the Constitution and constitutional reform process. They used radio and television as a medium to raise their issues supported by the production of posters, T-shirts, flyers, etc. Employing the three national languages, the coalition collectively sought to educate and share information about the draft constitution and the referendum, while developing an identifiable constituency. But tensions began accruing and in subtle ways the two processes began to divide women, according to their political allegiances.

> *…Actually the interesting thing … was the fact that the women's coalition had members from the MDC, but at the same time the coalition through its member organisations also had links with ZANU-PF, through MPs and commissioners, people were quick to categorise and that way it was so difficult…'*[190]

NCA Women and CCZ Women

Initially, we agreed that 'we were not going to talk CCZ, we were not going to talk NCA, we were going to talk women…'[191] and it was resolved that:

> *As an entity it would not form an alliance with either the NCA or the government's commission, but individuals and organisations with the coalition were free to do so … further the coalition will lobby and provide evidence to the*

---

188 Comprising a chairperson, core group and secretariat.
189 Conversant transcript.
190 Conversant transcript.
191 Conversant transcript.

NCA and the commission on gender issues.[192]

But these ideals only served to mask the deeper political polarisations within the country at the time and, perhaps inevitably, created fissures within the women's coalition:

> *If you were aligned to the NCA you were immediately perceived as being anti-government, if you were aligned to the CCZ you supported ZANU PF...*[193]

While women identified the fight for the entrenchment of women's rights as a common goal, there were multiple ways for achieving this. Those women who engaged in the state-sponsored process believed in the strategy of engagement, as one conversant pointed out: 'change is brought about not by resistance only; depending on the circumstances change can also be brought about through engagement as well.'[194]

But these women experienced their own frustrations within the lumbering state-sponsored process. The assault of a women commissioner by a fellow commissioner merely confirmed, in very tangible and real ways, the patriarchal power differentials. These were articulated by one conversant:

> *The Constitutional Commission? That was an experience and a half. As you know I experienced violence and have taken legal steps about that. We were there, we were asking for certain issues to do with the advancement of women but each time it was felt, 'Oh, these women again'... if they allowed anything to come in it was like they were doing us a favour, it was not our right to insist on these issues and the participation of women in communities, which was very poor. The one thing that became glaringly obvious working for the CCZ was that we have underestimated the degree of patriarchy in our society. Every single item concerning women in the CCZ had to be struggled for and it was not easy. For me now, it's understanding the subtle ways in which you can engage with power to your own advantage.*[195]

But while in the CCZ women were 'outnumbered by patriarchal men' making the situation 'impossible' and restricting the room for manoeuvre, those women who had aligned themselves to the more democratic NCA saw the need to

---

192 Minutes of the core group meeting of the Women's Coalition on the Constitution, 26 April 1999. The Coalition, after much heated debate, eventually took a decision against submitting evidence to the CCZ as it felt that this would endorse and validate a flawed and discredited process.

193 Conversant transcript.

194 Conversant transcript.

195 Conversant transcript.

maintain links and challenge civil society's patriarchal positionings. Women were consistently vocal about gender imbalances within the NCA and vigorously campaigned for better representation of women on the task forces.

This eventually met with victory at the NCA general assembly held in June 1999 where eight women, out of a possible eighteen were elected onto the task force.[196] Two months later as Chair-elect Morgan Tsvangirai stepped down to concentrate on the formation of a political party, and the NCA deputy chairperson, Thoko Matshe, then the Director of the ZWRCN, was unanimously supported to lead this civic alliance. Her assertive leadership style was clear:

Who am I beside my name and my position at my workplace? I am a feminist, without even a whiff of an apology for naming myself thus. I am an activist and a fearless fighter ... some people saw me as an outspoken woman and hence it seemed politically correct to have me in the lead. Others saw me as a soft option... who could be gently pushed off centre when the time was right... I think people completely misjudged me.[197]

Why was she elected? Among the reasons that could be offered, I suggest two: her maverick personality, and the need for the NCA to be seen as an alternative democratic space, of which the upholding of women's rights are an indicator. Whatever the reasons, having a woman from the women's movement as chair of a civic alliance meant that the the movement had been propelled into a role of prominence within civic organising:

In the year 2000 it was the NCA and the women's movement, and in both these spheres women were playing a pivotal role. So to a large extent the whole civic process was in the hands of the women's movement... during 1999 and 2000 we were very visible and I think our influence was felt directly. We had free reign where the NCA was censored in the media we had the space and we did what we liked. In fact we were quoted extensively. The media would call us the group of 13 because we were the 13 biggest women's organisations.[198]

This 'double militancy'[199] (Hellman 1992) meant that women were involved in both democratic and women's struggles: ideally one should influence the other.

---

196 44%. All elected women were members of the Coalition and included: Thoko Matshe; Mabel Sikhosana, Grace Kwinjeh, Lydia Zigomo, Yvonne Mahlunge.

197 Conversant transcript.

198 Conversant transcript.

199 Hellman, J. A. (1992). 'The study of new social movements in Latin America and the question of autonomy' in Alvarez, S. and A. Escobar (eds) in *The Making of Social Movement in Latin America*. Boulder CO: Westview Press.

> *It felt schizophrenic in a way, we were all juggling so many hats, but we were clear*
> *that when it came to the coalition it was about women, women, women first.[200]*

But the possibilities and limitations of this arrangement must also be acknowledged. In reality, civil society can be just as ossified and resistant to meaningful gender transformation as the state. Thoko Matshe asserts:

> *There was all sorts of political horse-trading within the NCA ... [but] knowing*
> *that the dirtiness of the game is what keeps most women out of politics, I knew I*
> *was going to stick in there, after all, the dirtiness was about the exercise of power*
> *... had I been male, being a substantive chair would never have been an issue for*
> *debate. But the positioning of women remains very contested.[201]*

YES or NO: The Referendum on the Constitution and the Women's Vote

The coalition's process of nation-wide consultation with women resulted in the production of a Women's Charter[202] in 1999, which would form the basis of future advocacy efforts. The optimism underlying this action is clear:

> *Perhaps we were naïve to think we could continue to experience this utopia where*
> *we don't get targeted. We were happy, we organised, we felt that women could be a*
> *kind of rallying point... the women's movement had a very direct impact on civil*
> *society and the politics of the day in 1999 and 2000.[203]*

While civil society groups like the NCA were severely policed and monitored to the extent that the state-controlled media were instructed not to carry any NCA material, the women's coalition appeared to have slipped the net. With access to the airwaves, they began a series of national civic education radio and television programmes.

A strong women's outreach, strategic civil society alliances, and a vocal group of women within state processes meant that the women's coalition had a constituency and multiple bases from which to influence the power differentials and thus constituted a force that could direct action.

The CCZ's draft constitution was put to a referendum in February 2000, and in its wake heated debate took place as to whether the women's coalition would call for a 'yes' or 'no' vote.[204] It was at this point that:

---

200 Conversant transcript.
201 Conversant transcript.
202 See Appendix 4.
203 Conversant transcript.
204 *Daily News*, 20 December 1999. 'Women's Groups Threaten to Reject Draft Constitution'.

The women's movement realised that they had gone way beyond what they had bargained for… we could no longer stay neutral, it was politics now, that was the game we were playing and there was no turning back, we had to take a side…[205]

It was then that the fissures finally cracked.

Many understandings co-exist as to what exactly transpired. Some member organisations articulated the need to remain 'apolitical' and maintain a women's agenda. Others believed that this was the opportunity to push for one that was transformative, and they supported the 'no' vote. Many women I spoke to talk about a 'direct or indirect backlash' or 'infiltration' by the state: the theory is that the women involved in the state-led processes or had ZANU-PF affiliations were 'sent back into the coalition carrying a new agenda to influence women to buy into the state-led process'.[206] But arguably a more fundamentalist infiltration also took place alongside a rising conservatism.

But after much posturing and political jockeying, the coalition eventually mobilised its constituency and called for a 'no' vote in the referendum arguing that among other things the draft constitution:

Did not contain rights of women to own and control land: live free from violence; basic health care, education, equal pay for equal work, social welfare and legal aid, and no equal representation in the electoral system or employment … it did not protect women from negative cultural practices … The people's views were generally ignored. They wanted a non-executive elected president with powers exercised in conjunction with some other state authority to avoid contestation of power in one person, that was not provided for; the people wanted the current president to step down when the new constitution came into force, that was not provided for; so many things, a cabinet of not more than fifteen ministries – the draft provides for one with an upper limit of twenty – the people wanted the president to be able to dissolve parliament only at the expiration of its five-year term, the draft provides for the president to dissolve parliament any time on certain grounds …[207]

Within the broader national scenario, a 'no' vote was a wake-up call to the state. It was the first time, ZANU-PF had been met with such vocal and overwhelming opposition. But the Women's Coalition was still to feel the reverberations of their intense political organising as the state rapidly sidelined the constitutional debate in preparation for the June 2000 parliamentary elections.

---

205 Conversant transcript.
206 Conversant transcript.
207 Conversant transcript.

2000 Parliamentary Elections

Women are disappointed at the decline in their representation in Zimbabwe's next parliament following the recent elections, describing the development as 'retrogressive'. Only thirteen women were elected out of 55 who had contested in the 120 constituencies. Seven seats went to the main opposition Movement for Democratic Change (MDC) and six to the ruling ZANU-PF (Zimbabwe African National Union - Patriotic Front). This is about 10 per cent representation, down from the previous 14 per cent.[208]

This is how independent newspapers captured women's experiences of the 2000 parliamentary elections in Zimbabwe. But the question is what are the underpinnings of this representation of events.

Riding high on the victory of the referendum, the Women's Coalition, embodying women's interests through a Women's Charter, recognised the radicalism of an agenda that brought women together across political divides. It sought to consolidate its position by voting women candidates into parliament.

We prepared for the parliamentary elections and we felt that another aspect of the constitution could be brought into the picture ... let's vote in women candidates and once they are there we would be able to assert pressure to raise our issues and debates within parliament.[209]

But experiences on this continent have shown us that it is not enough to have women in parliament, as numbers do not necessarily signify gender sensitivity.[210] Neither does it mean that this public forum is receptive to women's interests. As one conversant noted:

Life in parliament has been tough for the few women who have made it. Male parliamentarians quickly label and silence you.[211]

Undeterred, the coalition began to facilitate a clearly articulated women's political agenda through the endorsement and support for the 55 women candidates who were standing for parliamentary elections. Women came together

... The powers that be started to see women could be a force to be reckoned with, and not just a force to be reckoned with in terms of women's issues, but politically

---

208 The *Zimbabwe Independent*, June 2000.
209 Conversant transcript.
210 The 1995 parliamentary elections saw the largest number of women being elected into parliament. Of 150 MPs, seventeen were women, yet it was also during this period that women's rights were most under threat.
211 Conversant transcript.

we were a force because we were beginning to get women across political parties talking when the males in those parties didn't really want to. So we could become a place where people could negotiate and unify and that wasn't necessarily what people wanted, particularly around parliamentary elections.[212]

It was the first time in the history of Zimbabwe that a women's agenda had been articulated in this way. In May 2000 women from different political parties met to brainstorm how to beat their male counterparts at their own game.[213] As one conversant who attended this meeting noted:

Women buried their political differences for democratic justice. Every political party has been guilty of suppressing the rise of women within the ranks, paying lip service to affirmative action. Women are not out of this highly contested political race. We have another battle of our own – challenging men's dominance in politics.[214]

But the coalition was only as strong as its constituent parts and these were organisations: NGOs with structures, systems, responsibilities and areas of operation, which were already burdened by the pressures of intense political organising. They rarely had the means or the flexibility to engage with a rapidly changing national political landscape.

What you got were boards saying, wait, wait, wait. You are making us a target. Hold on, lets think about this, particularly where the boards themselves had party affiliations.[215]

There were vociferous internal debates within the coalition over amongst many issues: whether or not to accept reformist positions, accepting what little women were being given or pushing for more fundamental change (half a loaf is better than nothing at all); whether to vote for a woman simply because she was a woman, even though during election campaigns, some women candidates had turned a blind eye to violence or positively advocated for it.

Let us also not forget that such comments speak to generational issues, and to the diverse and changing perceptions of the relationships between state and civil society, not to mention gender politics. Many of the older women on NGO boards reflected the views of a time when:

A lot of the 80s activists were not used to confronting the establishment directly, now I think there is confusion, they were used to working with government not

---

212 Conversant transcript.
213 *Daily News*, 15 May 2000. 'Women Rally Together to Boost Participation in Civic Issues'.
214 Conversant transcript.
215 Conversant transcript.

against government. They have not adapted to the changes as the generations and struggles have evolved and we have failed to bridge the gap internally, so when things became critical they clamped down.[216]

Meanwhile a new generation of activists had come to the fore who were demanding and engaging in a more radical politics.

A collective anxiety around the meaning of politicised action existed. It was manifested through numerous boards of long-standing organisations,[217] who were in structural positions of power and suddenly found themselves 'exposed'. Board members began calling for a more circumscribed approach to coalition activities, curtailing affiliation and contributions to it whether because of ZANU-PF allegiances, donor commitments, issues of staff and organisational security or simply a diffuse fear and deep-seated anxiety of retribututin and retaliation by the state.

Indeed, state-sponsored violence against all political opponents, real and imagined, reared its ugly head. 'ZANU-PF and MDC entered into retaliatory battles and the police took little or no action for damage to property, assault, torture and death.'[218] Women did not go unscathed and were assaulted and beaten for their political affiliations.[219] There were numerous cases of MDC and ZANU women supporters being assaulted. Women who identified with the women's coalition through wearing headscarves or pins were also vulnerable. As were women contesting seats in the upcoming election. Nyasha Chikwinya, a ZANU-PF candidate, was assaulted and in a neck brace. Sekai Holland, a MDC candidate, was also the survivor of such an assault.

But these women also became victims of violence within their political parties. ZANU-PF's rural strongholds and MDC's urban following meant that those areas would go largely uncontested. And the logic that prevailed given this scenario, as one conversant noted:

Yes there was violence, mmm, yes, even within political parties women were exposed to violence. You have women colleagues actually attacked by male colleagues,[220]

---

216 Conversant transcript.

217 Like Musasa Project, ZWRCN and WAG.

218 See, Amnesty International report, Zimbabwe Terror Tactics in the run-up to Parliamentary Elections. July 2000, p. 8 and also Statement of the National Democratic Institute Pre-Election Delegation to Zimbabwe issued in Harare, 22 May 2000; Report of the Zimbabwe Human Rights Forum, Who is Responsible? A Preliminary Analysis of Pre-election Violence, June 2000.

219 See *The Standard*, 26 March 2000. 'Women Brave Violence to say No'.

220 Nyasha Chikwinya, ZANU-PF MP.

because they were challenging male sites of domination. There was jockeying by males within the parties who took safe seats leaving women candidates exposed in unsafe areas. Men will not automatically support us. It was fight for survival and men were protecting men and leaving the women out to dry. So there was violence from without, the violence that seized the nation, but also violence from within.[221]

In the face of this kind of violence the coalition found that it was unable to adequately support women: it had over-estimated its role and capacity:

The women's coalition, the women's movement, the broader base could not provide support. We had not organised, we had not thought around how to protect these women. Because you say to women stand, you say to women vote, you say to women campaign and then they become exposed, and when they were vulnerable we found ourselves unable to offer support.[222]

Many key organisations lost staff members during this period. Among the many reasons, one could point to the disjuncture between the visions of board members and staff; deepening national and socio-economic strife, also meant that in very real ways women sought more personal and financial security.

Women activists have been exposed, we've had threats some implied, some direct. We are doing some serious thinking, counting the costs. I am in the movement and I am prepared to sacrifice myself but what about those I am responsible to?[223]

In addition, this period of intense organising left many women activists exhausted and in need of time to recover and regroup. Thus it became a period of withdrawal, resignation and immigration.

As you can see all those strong organisations are without staff. Key people at WAG; Rhumbi left, ZWRCN, you left, Thoko left, Musasa is the same, a top layer of management and leadership has gone from these organisations…[224]

Thus, it is within this context, that one can place the discourse of a weakened and fragmented movement, as articulated at the Book Café discussion (see p.ix). There was a collective pause after the 2000 elections, and the intense activity and expectations, which had preceded them. Some conversants referred to the need to 'lie low' or to 'go underground' in the face of what was expected to be an even more violent presidential election in 2001.

The women's movement had found itself in a cul de sac, the meeting on 8

---

221 Conversant transcript.
222 Conversant transcript.
223 Conversant transcript.
224 Conversant transcript.

February 2001 can be intepreted as the first step towards a period of necessary reflection for the movement in Zimbabwe. I would now like to engage in some analytical reflections on this case-study. I once again reiterate that this reflection is the presentation of just one understanding and interpretation of this herstory.

Chapter 6

THEORETICAL CHALLENGES
IMPLICATIONS FOR THE MOVEMENT

I began this study with two objectives: to reconstruct a herstory of Zimbabwean women's collective action, and to examine the nature of this endeavour during the period 1995-2000. The construction of the scenario realises my first objective and significantly challenges malestream narratives that seem intent on disappearing women.[225] I turn therefore to my second objective. Here I will attempt to examine the nature of women's organisation and action in Zimbabwe and redefine the conceptualisation of a women's movement in a post-colonial context.

In Chapter 1, I asserted that there are theoretically contrasting views as to what constitutes a movement. In sum, however, the literature suggests that while it may be characterised by a diversity of interests, forms of expression and spatial locations, to speak of a movement implies:

A social or political phenomenon of some significance, that significance being given by numerical strength, but also by capacity to effect change in some way or another be it in legal, cultural or political terms.[226]

Such definitional bounds have contributed to ignoring or obscuring particular manifestation of movements and have precluded examining them in their own right. The Zimbabwean movement was neither a political nor social 'phenomenon'; it cannot be characterised by 'numerical strength', neither can it be held rigidly accountable for its ability to effect change. Yet in my view the question 'does Zimbabwe have a women's movement?' does not require a sustained

---

225 See Makumbe, Moyo and Raftopoulos, op.cit.
226 Molyneux, M. (1998). 'Analysing Women's Movements' in *Development and Change* 29 (2): 219.

polemic. Women who belonged to the many different organisations referred to herein, despite their different goals and experiences, could consciously or unconsciously be said to self-identify as a movement in Zimbabwe at this time, this collective consciousness means the movement exists through self-definition, however fragile and uneven it may be.

More importantly, however, the case testifies very powerfully to two decades (1980-2000) of sustained active engagement in gender-based struggles. One cannot ignore this. Thus instead of grappling with definitional bounds, I will examine the nature and form of the Zimbabwe women's movement.

Manifestations of a Movement

Molyneux suggests that the appearance and form of a women's movement are contingent on five factors:

> *Prevailing cultural configurations, family forms, political formations, the forms and degree of female solidarity and the character of civil society in the national context.*

In other words movements are processes that are shaped and modified by context. A movement is in a constant process of reflection, communication and negotiation as it defines and redefines itself. It is within this context that I would like to finally come to understand the meeting held at the Book Café on 8 February 2001.

> *You can interpret this as a moment when Zimbabwe is having to look at itself in ways that are critical, that are frightening. It's like a cul de sac, but cul de sac's are useful because they make you realise or make you aware that you need to turn around and in turning around look at yourself and in looking at yourself you can work your way out.*

> *The national context in Zimbabwe has not been easy to navigate, characterised, as it is, by authoritarianism, the flouting of the rule of law and all democratic principles, including respect for human rights. Covert and overt hostility to dissenting voices has meant that people live in fear. This, coupled with social and economic breakdown, has meant that in very real terms issues of safety and survival are tantamount. How has this context impacted on the movement?* [227]

Since 1980, there has been a powerful transformation in the way in which women's organisations have set their objectives, and worked together. This transformation has arisen out of a growing political consciousness of the nature of the many challenges women must confront.

---

227 Conversant transcript.

If we examine the Zimbabwean women's movement during the period under review what insight can we gain into its particular features? The movement is diffuse and fragmented, comprised of small, discrete, bounded groupings, organisations and individuals, that agree to come together for a specific purpose only to disband and reform in another constellation. This extemporaneous manifestation can be tracked from the cautious challenge to the PVO act, the robust interventions taken around the abrogation of constitutional rights,[228] through to more sustained actions around land advocacy and constitutional reform.

One can rightly ask, does a conservative state and a hostile political, social and economic environment necessarily spawn this particular type of response or manifestation of gender politics and struggle?[229] A more comprehensive comparative study needs be undertaken in other authoritarian or militarised environments in order to substantiate such a claim; but this is how the women's movement has manifested itself in Zimbabwe. One could argue that in the face of state hostility and the rapidly shrinking space for civil society organising,[230] this loose and flexible form of organisation was advantageous. It enabled women to operate in, as it were, the nooks and crannies, to continue to organise as bounded organisational entities, but also more subversively as a collective. For much of the 1990s, this strategy allowed the movement to continue its activities 'unnoticed by the state' precisely because it was not perceived as a threat or a consolidated site of power.

The culmination of this serendipitous manifestation of women's organising lies in the formation of the women's coalition in 1999. This was a strategic intervention on the part of the movement at a time when it's potential to inform and shape national debate required both consolidation and mobilisation. It was an action that drew on rich experience, and a cultivated constituency, which displayed fairly sophisticated refinement of a strategy. But consolidation meant more visibility; the coalition became a political site where power accrued. Thus it became open to attack by those forces that were jockeying for power, both within the realm of civil society and the state.

In this instance, women came under attack, not solely because they were

---

228 See particularly the campaigns around Amendment 14, Magaya vs Magaya, Stripping of women in the streets.

229 Mama, A. in her 1999 essay 'Dissenting Daughters?' poses a similar type of question in her examination of the women's movement in a military state. p 31.

230 In the period 2000-08 there was growing political, economic and social instability in Zimbabwe.

women advocating a certain agenda, but because they were perceived as political players with the ability to influence and direct the course of action whilst maintaining a clearly articulated 'women's agenda'. More significantly, women began to see themselves as a political force. This is a radical change, one that requires a re-conceptualisation of what it means to be a woman activist for social justice, because women have not had a traditional engagement with the state as a political site in this way before.

The Movement versus the State

The literature attests[231] and my analysis confirms that the state provided the central impetus to women's organising in the period 1995-2000. This resulted in a somewhat inchoate engagement as the case demonstrates, and as is characteristic of women's movements in other African contexts. Manuh[232] in her analysis of relations between women, society and the state under PNDC rule in Ghana; Tsikata's[233] work on women's political organisations in Ghana; Mama[234] writing on Nigeria, and Tamale[235] writing on Uganda, come to similar conclusions. These studies all raise questions about the 'likelihood of existing organisational forms challenging women's oppression or advancing women's political, social or economic interests.'[236]

But the Zimbabwean case provides a counterpoint to this statement by demonstrating the mergence of new kinds of political strategy. The actions taken by the Women's Coalition with regard to constitutional reform showed that the women's movement was in a strong position to determine and take forward both a national and a women's agenda. No matter its successes or failures, this cannot be discounted; rather, the Zimbabwe case tells us a great deal about context and strategy and the lessons we can learn from this. In this vein, I would like to explore how women's understanding of the state in Zimbabwe has profoundly

---

231 Tsikata, D. (1999). 'Gender Equality and the State in Ghana: Some Issues of Policy and Practice'. In Imam, A. et al. *Engendering African Social Sciences*. Dakar: CODESRIA. Mama, A. 1999. Dissenting Daughters? Gender Politics and Civil Society in a Militarised State in CODESRIA Bulletin 3 & 4.

232 Manuh, T. (1993). 'Women, the State and Society under the PNDC' in Gyimah-Boadi, E. *Ghana under PNDC Rule*. Dakar: CODESRIA.

233 Tsikata, D. (1999) op. cit.

234 Mama, A. (1999) op. cit.

235 Tamale, S. (1999). *When Hens Begin to Crow: Gender and Parliamentary Politics in Uganda*. Boulder: Westview Press.

236 Mama, A. (1996). *Women's Studies and Studies of Women in Africa During the 1990s*. Dakar: CODESRIA, p. 19.

shaped the form and content of their activism.

The Zimbabwean case explodes the structuralist perception of the state as a monolithic entity. Instead, it offers support for feminist and post-structuralist theorisations that see the state as a highly complex and contested terrain (see Chapter 1), comprised not only of a president, but cabinet ministers, the legal system, law enforcement agents, constituted commissions, discourses, and institutions, which all come together to constitute it. But the state is also a shorthand term to describe a 'network of power relations existing in co-operation and also in tension with and against each other'.[237] This conceptualisation of a multiplicity of sites demands, by its very nature, a variety of strategies and action to take an agenda forward. The extent to which the Zimbabwe women's movement has understood and fully exploited this conceptualisation of the state is debateable.

In the main, the movement has viewed the state as an arbiter of development and a bestower of rights. This is evidenced firstly through the movement's fixation on asking, challenging, and appealing to the state to enshrine rights. Secondly, advocacy has demanded an expansion in the roles of the state through the provision of services and the establishment of frameworks that mitigate gendered impacts[238] and ensure gender equality. In this way it is seen to be integral to the securing of women's rights. But what is wrong with this picture?

It is contradicted by a movement that sees itself in opposition to the state as a patriarchal, hostile and conservative structure. Operation Clean-Up is an early example of this tendency. But it can be corroborated over time through the blatant retraction of rights as evidenced in the Magaya vs Magaya case, remaining silent in the face of rampant gender-based violence, including the stripping of women in the streets or by offering women little access to ownership of land or means of production under the guise of what is or is not 'culturally appropriate'.

This contradictory scenario has established a pattern in which women make demands upon the state for the securing of rights; these are either endorsed or rejected depending on the state's own agenda and interests. At certain moments the state has 'allowed' progressive legislative reform that entrenched women's rights. But at other moments when its own position was threatened or compromised, in times of economic crisis or moral panic, these came under threat of

---

237 Rai, S. (1996). 'Women and the State in the Third World: Some issues for Debate' in Rai, S. and Lievesley, G. (eds) (1996). *Women and the State: International Perspectives*. London: Taylor Francis.

238 Hassim, S. (1991). 'Gender, Social Location and Feminist Politics in South Africa' in *Transformation* 15.

retraction. The Legal Age of Majority Act and the abrogation of rights gained through the Administration of Estates Bill through the Magaya vs Magaya ruling can be sited as examples. This contradictory experience would make it difficult to sustain a unitary conceptualisation of the state.

In light of this, the wisdom in zoning in and fixating solely on rights and legal reform comes into question. As one conversant points out:

> *It seems a pity that 15-20 years after the existence of some of these organisations, we still peddle the falsity that the answer lies in the law. You can demand from the state laws from A-Z but it will not work, we've seen it. Our battle is in fact not with the law per se, our struggle is with patriarchy.*[239]

There is much debate on whether women should pursue legal reforms within the state or stay outside of it. Some groups believe that effective reform can only come through the state[240] while others argue that the state co-opts women's issues pointing to ways in which new legislation, which seemingly favours women, has afforded the state – not women – more power.[241] Alvarez, and Jaquette[242] take both sides of the argument into account when they argue for more pragmatism in working selectively with the state while maintaining an awareness of its limitations. What is clear is that in the process of negotiation and engagement with the state, not only do women's agendas get ignored, blocked or watered down, but women themselves get co-opted into state machinations be it through personal, professional or political allegiances and interests. In this way the state allows certain leverage, a certain space for radical dissenting voices, but it doesn't allow them to become consolidated.

Civil Society and the Women's Movement

Just as the movement has made demands upon the state it has also sought out allies who were often drawn from larger Zimbabwean civil society. Activism around the PVO Act, land and constitutional reform are examples of such alliances. While the scope of this study does not allow for an in-depth analysis of civil society, I would like to spend some time exploring this site in relation to its implications for women's organising. My reasons for doing this are twofold.

239 Conversant transcript.

240 See Alverez, S. E. (1990). *Engendering Democracy in Brazil.* Princeton NJ: Princeton University Press.

241 See Ghandi, N. and Shah, N. (1991). *The Issues at Stake: Theory and Practice in Contemporary Women's Movement in India.* New Delhi: Kali for Women.

242 Alvarez (1990) op. cit., Jaquette, J.S. (ed.), 1989. *The Women's Movement in Latin America: Feminism and the transition of democracy.* Boston: Unwin Hill Hyman.

Firstly, the women's movement is an example of a civil society grouping and should be examined within its broader context. Secondly, civil society in Zimbabwe has come to be understood as a key and important force in the push for a democratic dispensation, to the extent that civil society, and the organisations and political parties it has spawned, notably the NCA and MDC, have been held up as the 'alternative' to ZANU-PF.

Civil Society in Zimbabwe is an umbrella term comprising of amongst other agents: the trade union movement, student activists, churches, anti-capitalist and socialist groupings, human rights and women's movements, academics and political commentators, the media and development activists. By its very composition, it too is heterogeneous and also includes multiple and competing agendas. Within an authoritarian national context, the harsh reality is that civil society structures are very fragile and have limited reach and capacity.

Leadership tends to draw from privileged classes bent on maintaining the status that they have heavily invested in. Paradoxically, this privilege has often accrued from earlier association with the state. The civil society sector is reliant on external funding and this too places it in a precarious position regarding sustainability and the ability to wage an autonomous struggle. The women's movement typifies these key features (see Chapter 3). But these realities do not imply that civil society cannot create some political space for democratising forces and provide a platform for critical reflection that informs activism. It does, however, point to the very real limitations of capacity, which render it unable to transform systemic conditions and take full advantage of the gap created by a 'rolled back' state.[243]

One would think that civil society would be a more receptive recipient and conduit of a gender agenda than the state. But it is something of a political tragedy that broader civil society, increasingly assumed to be the voice of democracy and progressive principles, did not instinctively at any time rise up to protest blatant violations of women's rights in the period under review. Where was civil society when women were being stripped naked on the streets, where were they when women were being dispossessed of property or when they were waging struggle for the enshrinement of fundamental property rights? They were silent. This silence I would argue was due to an inability to transcend patriarchal tradition of political engagement.

---

243 As argued by Bratton, M. (1994). 'Civil Society and Political Transitions in Africa' in *Civil Society and the State in Africa* (eds) Harbeson, J. W., Rothchild, D. and Chazan, N. Boulder: Lynne Rienner Publishers

It is only around constitutionalism that the alliance between women and broader civil society was cemented. This could be bluntly explained as being borne of instrumentalism; that the NCA needed women to legitimise their agenda to secure donor funding, and strategically and politically to draw in a local constituency. The fact is that women still had to wage a struggle within the NCA (Chapter 5) in order for gender concerns to be meaningfully taken up. More crucially, this signifies the depth of crisis within a sphere that lays claim to the status of being progressive and enlightened but that often does not recognise the rights of women as goals within themselves.

An even more disturbing comparison can be drawn between the NCA, the MDC and the nationalist movement. Both the MDC and NCA argued that the crisis in Zimbabwe was primarily due to the current regime. According to them, the regime had to be ousted before any other issues could be addressed. History has illustrated how dangerous just such an argument is for women. Thus, as one conversant noted, the ultimate struggle is indeed against patriarchy.

Women are located both within the state and civil society. The movement has never had enough power, volume or force to effect major social and political changes on its own, so it has had to form alliances to push its agenda forward. This means that the women's movement exists across the state and civil society as women within the movement are located within and have allegiances to these two spheres. Neither site is ideal for the furthering of the movement's agenda, but both offer opportunities for engagement that need to be weighed and assessed strategically to ensure that women's agendas are furthered and not co-opted or over-turned. In this context how do women articulate their agenda and formulate their interests?

In Chapter 1, I used Molyneux's work to raise the issue of women's interests in collective action. In order to move my discussion on the Zimbabwean women's movement forward and deepen my analysis, I would like to revisit the concepts here. Molyneux argues that whatever form female mobilisation has taken, it has always expressed demands for full citizenship and rights and has highlighted women's everyday strength and ability to pursue their interests in the public sphere. She goes on to suggest that the formulation of interests, whether they are practical or strategic, is intrinsically linked to identity formation. 'Thus women's interests are subject to cultural, historical and political variation.'[244]

If one looks at the concept of women's interests from this vantage, it be-

---

244 Molyneux M. (1998). p. 233.

comes more complex. Complex because women's interests are no longer based solely on objective needs. By centering political identity in this way, one can ask, what subjective sense of self motivates women to act and make certain demands at particular points in time. Thus interests may be linked to notions of power and the multiple inflections that shape the post-colonial subject, which include gender, race, class and ethnicity.

With this inflection it is erroneous to think that the terrain of the Zimbabwean women's movement is all encompassing or that women's interests are uniform. To a certain extent the movement has seen itself as fairly homogenous, and this has been reflected in the fact that discourses and discussions on internal differences and diversities have been glaringly absent. Instead, it has defined itself within a liberal human-rights-based agenda that has further contributed to the masking of internal diversity.

> *We were clear that we needed to articulate a women's agenda, women came together. It was about women. This was the only way to take our issues forward.*[245]

The deference to rights means that at one level woman do have a collective voice and position leading to unity in action. Women were questioning everything.

> *The issues were raised through the consultative civic education process around the constitution. We were talking about equality and the removal of discrimination: property and land rights, the legal age of majority act, customary law, rights to education, women's participation in decision-making, health and reproductive health rights, the whole election process, gender-based violence, issues of poverty, international human rights instruments and mechanisms for the enforcement of rights.*[246]

But once again it is not as simple as this. The movement is comprised of organisational forms, each with their own modus operandi, particular goals and visions. At another it is comprised of individuals who, while they may all be women, embody diverse historical and political experience. As one conversant points out:

> *If you look at the women's movement it is broad and open and every Jane, Jill and Susan will come in. But if you make a mistake and assume that its open terrain is a political space that reflects your principles, no, it doesn't work like that. Women themselves in the movement are not homogenous and so their politics reflects the diversity.*[247]

---

245 Conversant transcript.
246 Conversant transcript. In reference to Women and the Zimbabwean Constitution: A Fact Sheet. ZWRCN, 1999.
247 Conversant transcript.

So, in fact, there is a disturbingly precarious, almost imaginary sense of consensus within the movement. The diversity of views, strategies and opinions have repeatedly manifested at critical moments: around land invasions, the yes/no vote at the time of the referendum on the constitution, and the movement has experienced fracturings along those very same lines. As one conversant noted:

> *There were meetings around constitutional reform where we literally wanted to throw each other out of the window, it was so bad. It trashed the whole sisterhood thing, you know, it was like getting hit in the face with cold water. Like, this is reality; because for those of us who have been in the movement we always felt that it does not matter what kind of differences we might have, but a sister is a sister. We are bound to gel at some point. But the stark reality is that it was about politics now, it was a repositioning.[248]*

This understanding unequivocally points to a movement whose agenda is constantly being internally contested, because women bring different subjectivities, which inform their political identities, to the table. It is neither homogeneous, nor open, but rather a site at which very many different agendas come into play. The critical questions remain: who comprises it, shapes the politics and defines the direction and the vision; and who neutralises the critical elements and radical voices?[249] At the heart of these variant voices lies the issue of gender politics.

Thus I move into the realm of the invention of political identities within the movement and I would like to argue that at the centre of this inability to face its own diversity resides the fact that the movement has not, until the point in 1999-2000, conceptualised itself as a political force. Gender politics within women's movements is something that has not yet been adequately explored in the literature; but based on the Zimbabwean case, I would like to suggest that it is an aspect which is crucial to the shape and definition of a movement.

An Exploration of Gender Politics

The detailed documentation of the growth and development of women's organising in Zimbabwe[250] presented here, provides a basis for identifying the various strands of gender politics contained under the rubric of the Zimbabwe women's movement. For the purposes of this critique I identify certain political orientations and describe them in order to highlight this point. In reality, however, the

248 Conversant transcript.
249 Often criticising them as xenophobically or homophobically western and foreign.
250 See Chapter 4.

manifestation of a political orientation is by no means fixed or static, rather these positionings are constantly contested and in flux.

Molyneux suggests that the distinction between practical and strategic gender interests helps us differentiate between ways of reasoning about gender relations and thus allows us to 'see' gender politics. Molyneux suggests that:

> *In the formulation of practical interests there is the assumption that there is com-*
> *pliance with the existing gender order, while in the case of strategic interests there is*
> *an explicit questioning of that order and of the compliance of some women with it.*
> *Such a distinction between what Gramsci called a practical consciousness and what*
> *we could term a strategic vision has always been important to politics, especially*
> *to emancipatory politics. How else, other than through what Foucault calls 'the*
> *critical labour of thought upon itself', could claims to think differently, and to see*
> *the world in different terms to that which is presented in conventional stories about*
> *social relations, occur? If, in the formulation of practical interests, women take*
> *inequality or male authority over them for granted, then this is a different way of*
> *seeing the world to that which evolves in the course of political discussion premised*
> *on alternative, egalitarian visions. If feminism, like other forms of critical theory,*
> *insists on seeing this reality as containing oppressive relations and social injustices,*
> *and if its practice is concerned with challenging and changing it, then it depends on*
> *some measure of critical, alternative thought and hence on some means of making*
> *value judgements about the social order.*[251]

These 'value judgements' often resulted in contradictory and incompatible positions within a movement, which did not talk about its own politics and diversity, and this has gone a long way to contributing to its own fragility. Women's political reticence in Zimbabwe has translated into coexisting discourses that are contested on a daily basis in deciding what organisations and coalitions will and will not do. While the scope of this work does not allow me to fully explore the development and implications of women's political identities it certainly provides the seeds for future work and theorisation. Manifestations of gender politics could be traced throughout the research process via conversants understandings and positionings in relation to events that took place within the movement.

I have pointed out (Chapter 4) that the decade after independence saw the birth of many women's organisations established by women who had close links to the ruling party either through direct involvement in state structures or through a history of the nationalist liberation struggle. The focus of these

---

251 Molyneux, M. op.cit. p. 235/236.

organisations, clubs and income-generation activities supported women's reproductive roles and left gender relations largely untouched, in this way reinscribing
and supporting the patriarchal status quo, even if unconsciously so. The discourses that emanated out of this period of organising were largely welfarist in
their orientation drawing from WID and WAD paradigms in direct support of
the state's policy of reconstruction and development. They were nationalist or
reformist political positionings and can be characterised by an understanding of
effecting change from within, an engagement with state structures and processes
and an implicit understanding that gender rights and discourses will be bestowed
within the parameters of what the state will allow. How did this operate? In the
words of one conversant:

> *I remember the energies of Zimbabwe women when Mugabe said, 'Women don't*
> *get married if you want to own property'. And I remember someone saying 'Who*
> *does he think he is, is he God Mugabe?' I was amazed, yes, yes continue, fight on,*
> *sister. But always somebody would stand up and a few other voices would say, 'Well*
> *you know we are not here to attack the state, the government is not our enemy and*
> *neither are men.' Always those moderate, neutralising voices and they were the ones*
> *who had the legitimacy.*[252]

Thus you had a muzzled discourse and hovering unease about contestation
with the state in terms of rights and entitlement. Neutralising voices that would
invariably surface at those crucial points of possible confrontation with the state.
Another example of this is embedded within the yes/no debate at the time of
the referendum when women supporting state-led process were viewed as col-
laborators.

> *They mobilised the women through the constitutional process and then pushed them*
> *back into the movement carrying a new agenda. They did it very well and these*
> *women came into the coalition saying well let's accept the draft of the CCZ because*
> *it secures some rights, half a loaf of bread is better than nothing at all.*[253]

In the early post-independence years we see clearly articulated feminist discourses and the birth of a set of organisations rooted in a feminist ideology and
agenda (Chapter 4). These discourses were based on the recognition of patriarchy as a system of male oppression and domination, which sought a holistic and
structural transformation of society and relationships. This vision was embodied
by women who were self-proclaimed 'outed' feminists. However, in the face of

---

252 Conversant transcript.
253 Conversant transcript.

an increasingly hostile state, where the assault on women gradually meant that even past gains seemed precarious, the movement quickly began to distance itself from an 'overt' feminist politics.[254] Feminist politics is not an easy politics and as one conversant noted:

Feminism in this country died … because Zimbabwean women were not ready to defend feminism. They did not realise how critical feminist thinking and energies were for the bigger movement. They backed off. I remember a leader of a key women's organisation telling me, 'it's too hot an issue'.[255]

By the mid-1990s one saw the disappearance of the words 'oppression' and 'exploitation', 'patriarchy' and 'feminism' from the movements' lexicon. It is revealing when one considers the terms that seem to have replaced them: 'gender' and 'mainstreaming'. These moves to 'disappear' feminism, as an articulated discourse framing women's activism and actions, could have been presented as 'strategic' to ensure that the spaces for organising remained open – although this is debatable, and the move has not been articulated as such. Feminism was constructed as too inflammatory. It required naming yourself in a way that could not be easily accommodated by the collective national psyche, nor indeed by some women within the movement.

A decade later (1990s) feminist voices remained muted, and there was an embracing of a more acceptable 'gender sensitivity' or gender planning dictum; a hegemonic technical discourse about framing praxis. This was a discourse already articulated by international donors and framed by a host of international women's human rights instruments and national frameworks of which the Beijing Platform for Action was then the most current.[256] The availability of donor aid[257] in support of work within the 'gender and development' paradigm supported this, and the subsequent bevy of organisations to which it gave rise. These organisations found the articulation of gender and development discourses under the rubric of the United Nations[258] and a series of global International

---

254 An example of which was the closure of the Feminist Studies Centre due to state intervention and the tensions that accrue around feminism and feminists in Zimbabwe.

255 Conversant transcripts.

256 In Zimbabwe women activist were referred to as Beijing.

257 It is important to note that not all donors are alike, and that donor funding of NGOs in Zimbabwe does not necessarily imply a totalitarian hold over the activities therein. External interventions through funding are not always imperial, and not always counterproductive. Sometimes insubordination by both donors and recipients, is behind much of the creativity in Women's NGOs and Zimbabwean civil society more generally.

258 Mexico City, 1975; Nairobi, 1985; Beijing 1995.

Instruments, including CEDAW:[259] thus, a relatively safer discursive haven for furthering women's equality, as well as a means of providing more leverage for a women's agenda. In this way a developmental gendered politics emerged and gained ascendance over more radical feminist voices.

Gender was increasingly being promoted and used by the World Bank, the UN, bilateral agencies, civil society, and the Zimbabwean government, all of whom were linking the concept to development assistance. At this time, the movement saw many women take up a more technocratic gendered discourse in servicing these sites, as consultants. One needs, however, to guard against the language of development agencies taking over the voices of political struggle in this way. A major drawback to this unified global language is that it obscures the triangulation of power between governments, development-aid institutions and local activism; and it waters down the critical political edge.

Women within organisations forged links with donors, the state and civil society and these links were used to further women's collective action if the situation demanded it. Alliances were formed with ZANU-PF women MPs who at times attempted to push for a women's agenda, and attempted to massage the bounds of the party line, in the face of its rigidity.[260]. Similarly, various members of the movement were drawn into state processes at different times as commissioners, consultants, advisors and friends[261] of senior government officials. Donor alliances enabled women's NGOs to make certain kind of demands, even though they were reformist, under the gender and development and rights framework. This period saw the emergence and deployment of creative advocacy and lobbying strategies, which included multiple engagements across various sites, both within the state, donor community and civil society, in an attempt to further a women's agenda. But this period also saw very real clashes between competing discourses and politics.

It would seem, nonetheless, that the syncretic outcome of these contestations led to the emergence of a more tempered kind of radicalism. While a clearly articulated feminist discourse was muzzled, the issues being pushed and the strategies employed continued to speak to some kind of feminist underpinnings. The Women's Charter[262] as a clearly feminist articulation is just one example of this. Women's persistent challenge to patriarchy through the demands for entitlement,

---

259 Zimbabwe ratified CEDAW in 1991. However, it is enforceable through an Act of Parliament.
260 See for example The Administration of Estates Act 1996
261 Formally and even informally.
262 *See Appendix 4.*

the formulation of a women's agenda and the need to take this forward through women's political representation can all be cited as part of a transformatory agenda informed by a feminist vision.

I would like to suggest that during the period under review more radical forms of developmental feminism emerged somewhat serendipitously. Organisations and individuals implemented gender-focused developmentalist programmes within an institutionalised framework. This organisational base, although well funded, was bounded and constrained by systems, structures, government policy and donor demands. But this very same constrained organisational platform created the possibility for radicalism in the interstices. It allowed for women to create their own space, the Women's Coalition, to come together, pool their knowledge, skills and resources, and formulate and implement their own more autonomous agenda. So while organisations formed the bedrock, it was within the free spaces that one witnesses the real potential, the energies and lifeblood of the movement.

The strong potential for a transformatory politics, whether articulated as clearly feminist or not, still exists. It is this radical political voice that won out at the time of the referendum. It is fuelled by vibrant and dynamic regional and continental feminist discourses. Its proponents are resourceful and visibly influential and well-placed women who have a direct and clear political consciousness, being not only aware of women's oppression, but also prepared to actively confront patriarchal power in all its manifestations to address that oppression.

In a country as polarised as Zimbabwe it is easy to romanticise or dismiss a movement for its inability to secure meaningful change. The reality is more nuanced. If we are going to judge a movement by its inability to enshrine, protect and preserve the rights of women, then yes, the movement fails. But if we use an alternative lens, one that views struggle as process, one that sees the struggle as moving forward incrementally over time, one that is constantly contesting, negotiating webs of power whilst chipping away at the patriarchal foundations, then a complex and interesting scenario unfolds. It is a scenario that reveals exciting potential for women's activism in Zimbabwe.

The continued high levels of women's engagement in national politics suggests that the Zimbabwean women's movement is at the cutting edge of a new politics. It has ruptured liberal discourse and subverted, as an empty claim, the myth that everyone is fully represented in the discourses and practices that define who is a citizen and who has rights in Zimbabwe. Women are challenging the traditional relationships that accrue around property, and the accumulation and ownership of wealth, as it is linked to autonomy. Spheres that have been dominated by men are being contested and women are demanding the entitlements that mark them as full citizens.[263] The women's movement has not only worked to change the relationship between women and civil society, but they have also challenged relations with the state. They are overthrowing the construction of women as cultural custodians and therefore private/state-owned territories, which embody national identity. It is in the attempt to maintain an unequal relationship of power, in particular with reference to women's demands for securing of rights, that the state allows for misogynist practices. As one conversant noted:

> *The African women's movement is not only the most exciting movement to emerge from the 20th century as a century of nationalism and nationalist resistance but it is also really at the cutting edge of a new politics. The women's movement is very central to crafting a new politics, a post-colonial politics and this is very central to the vibrancy of the women's movement because we are overturning everything.[264]*

This has major implications for theory. In effect we are seeing a manifestation of a new form and strategies of a women's movement within a post-colonial African context and this study demonstrates the way in which reflection on praxis can usefully inform the development of new theories.

What the Women's Coalition did was revolutionary: it placed women in a powerful political 'space', one that traversed organisational interests and boundaries, and one that until then they had always been reluctant to occupy and claim. This resulted in a realisation of the primacy of gendered political positionings within the movement in strategising for change. It resulted in strategic alliances with broader civil society; it also ruptured old ways of understanding of the state. Now women were forced to confront the state as a political agent. Despite the contestation, the Women's Coalition allowed women to make the leap and articulate a women's politics based on women's interests. This is a manifestation of a different conceptualisation of politics, what I would like to call a post-colonial women's politics.

---

263 Full economic social and political rights.
264 Conversant transcript.

APPENDICES

1. A Snapshot of the Period under Review   83

2. List of Women Conversants   91

3. Bibliography   95

4. The Zimbabwe Women's Charter   101

Appendix 1: Snapshot of the Period (1995 – 2000)

Global trends

- UN's 2nd decade for women culminates in the Beijing World Conference on Women and the adoption of the Beijing Platform for Action.
- Donor presence and support for a gender agenda.
- World Bank and International Monetary Fund regulate economic growth through Economic Structural Adjustment and conditionalities on loans.

National Political & Socio-Economic Context	Civil Society Context	National Machinery & Policy Context	Women's Movement
• Focus on economic liberalisation. Macro-economic policy orientated to achieve economic growth, reduce public deficit and bring down inflation. • The effects of ESAP, the introduction of investment incentives and the removal of price controls translate into high inflation, rising debt, corruption amongst top government officials, growing unemployment, all exacerbating poverty. • Introduction of a safety net in the form of the social dimensions fund to mitigate the effects of ESAP.	• Evolution of a new group of NGOs[1] which attempt to professionalise operations whilst seeking accountability to their as yet weak constituencies. • Heavy reliance on donor funding. • In conditions of increasing poverty as a result of ESAP NGOs more willing to make a more frontal political assault on the state over issues of democratisation. • Attempts at developing NGO coalitions and advocacy around major policy issues[2] premise: collectivity = impact.	• Women's unit in Ministry of National Affairs Employment Creation and Co-operatives promotes activities aimed at enabling women to participate in and at all political levels and structures.[3] • 22 women MPs out of 150 elected. 96% ZANU stalwarts. • With major state cutbacks gender becomes sacrificed in national budget allocation. • With cutbacks in social spending and in the face of rising poverty and unemployment the unit is tasked with ensuring the availability of adequate social services to women.	• Increasingly hostile national circumstances re-assertion of patriarchy through the abrogation of gains. • Still limited by capacity and weak in terms of power and influence in making demands from the state. • Women's Organisations turn to: lobbying and advocacy for policy and legislative reform, gender training and education as more strategic interventions. • Increase in networking with a broader base of non-state actors. • Women's activism included long-term campaigns on land, legal reform, rights and health issues, coupled with efforts on issues like the defence of the Legal age of Majority Act.

Snapshot of the Period (1995 – 2000)

Global trends
N/A

National Polit-ical & Socio-Eco-nomic Context	Civil Society Context	National Machinery & Policy Context	Women's Movement
• General elections see ZANU-PF regain an overwhelming majority. • Mugabe elected for 3rd Presidential term with a 32% vote. • Passing of the Private Voluntary Organisations Act.[4] • Growth and consolidation of a black elite and an indigenisation business agenda. • Land redistribution programme implemented on recommendations from the Presidential Land Tenure Commission. State designates and purchases farms constrained by a lack of resources. • Under pressure through an ineffective land programme the state makes a unilateral decision to award war veterans a gratuity and monthly pension totalling Z$7 billion in compensation for their participation in the war of liberation.	• NGOs mobilise against the PVO Act imposed upon them by the State. The Act allowed for the suspension of any or all activities of an NGO.[5] • Zimbabwe Congress of Trade Unions becomes a stronger and consolidated force. • ZCTU initiates and leads mass action in the form of strikes, go-slows and national stayaways against price hikes, the introduction of arbitrary taxes and levies, human rights abuses. • Growth and consolidation of an independent print media. • Increased concern over human rights abuses. • National Constitutional Assembly mooted in 1996. Seeking to build a broad alliance of civic organisations around constitutional reform.	• The MNAECC unit responsible for establishing gender desks in all line ministries as mainstreaming is emphasised. • Unit experiences staffing inadequacies, structural constraints and gross under funding. • The units understanding of its role, the scope and scale of its activities and the lack of political will means the realisation of its goals are near impossible. • The state fails to address gender issues in any sustainable way.	• The implications of the PVO Act are brought home to the NGO community through the case of the Association of Women's Clubs (AWC). • AWC executive committee gazetted in November 1995. Organisation closed. The gazetted women take their case to the Supreme court in May1996 and in their affidavits challenge the legality of the section under whose terms they had been charged. • Despite vociferous efforts by women activists to push for the securing of land rights, the state remains unmoving in its consideration regarding women's access to and control over land. • Women form a lobby network to focus and co-ordinate land advocacy and activities.

Snapshot of the Period (1995 – 2000)

Global trends

- Increased WB and IMF pressure for stringent economic control in the face of spiralling inflation.
- Donor nervousness over increasing national instability. Many donors retract on aid programmes.

National Political & Socio-Economic Context	Civil Society Context	National Machinery & Policy Context	Women's Movement
• Pluralist party politics sees more than 20 weak oppositional political parties posing no threat to the status quo. • With soaring inflation and the depreciation of the Z$ mass stayaways. Politically motivated Food riots break out and accompanying clashes with law enforcement agents. • The state counters demonstrations the unleashing of law enforcement agents including the army display unprecedented force on civilians perpetrating gross human rights abuses. • Zimbabwe pledges support to the Laurent Kabila regime in the Congo sending troops at a cost of US$ 27 million a month. • Shortages of foreign currency and petrol.	• NCA holds a series of provincial meetings in trying to decentralise from Harare, in order to make its presence felt[6] and begin to establish national structures. • This period sees increasing demonstrations and rising discontent over a broad range of issues from rising food prices to corruption and human rights abuses. • A men's gender forum, locally known as Padare is formed to promote gender-sensitive attitudes and behaviours.[7] • NCA begins to gain momentum and support as they begin to prepare for an all-stakeholders conference.	• The President appoints Minister of Gender in the President's office.[8]	• Early 1997 Federation of Zimbabwean Women[9] mooted and launched, but it is unable to sustain itself. • With pressure from women activists, the Administration of Estates Amendment Act (1997) is passed which allows surviving spouses and children of the deceased in a customary law marriage to inherit property. Although it still provided the possibility for discrimination against women in polygamous unions, this landmark law allowed women in customary unions to inherit from their husbands and have recourse to the law in issues of inheritance.

Snapshot of the Period (1995 – 2000)

Global trends
• UK and the US relations with Zimbabwe strained.
• International feminist community come out in support of women's rights to property in solidarity at the time of the Magaya vs Magaya case.

National Political & Socio-Economic Context	Civil Society Context	National Machinery & Policy Context	Women's Movement
• In the face of civic debate and activism on the constitution the state feels its role is being usurped. • In mid-1999 it embarks on a constitutional reform exercise[10] and establishes a 395 member constitutional commission.[11] (13%), 52 members of which are women. • CCZ begins public hearings around the country gathering evidence in preparation to write a draft "home grown constitution".	• With numerous stakeholder meetings,[12] public forums and demonstrations, NCA continues with its process of gathering people's views with the intent of writing a draft constitution. • Alliances begin to form between the trade union movement and broader civil society actors as the leader of the Labour Movement is elected to chair the NCA.	• Unit attempts to complement the efforts of Women's NGOs but severely under resourced. • New Minister of Gender responsible for monitoring mainstreaming of gender in government ministries. In effect evaluating the role of the women's unit within MNAECC. • Some see this as an indication of the importance of gender on the national agenda, others as an indication of a weakening. Communication lines become blurred between the 2 structures and ministers.	• Organisations continue to come together to collectively advocate on issues that impact negatively on women's lives. Amongst others HIV/AIDS, Citizenship rights (amendment 14) inheritance issues, Gender based violence and constitutional reform are key. • 1997 Administration of Estates Act challenged by the 1999 Magaya vs. Magaya ruling. Supreme Court rules that under customary law women have no rights to property. International outrage. • Women's activism begins to focus solely on the constitution as the largely male NCA seemingly fails to initially provide a space for women.

Snapshot of the Period (1995 – 2000)

Global trends
- The international community begins to back the MDC.
- International journalists are barred from reporting on Zimbabwe.
- International election observers are split as to whether the Parliamentary election was free and fair.·
- Zimbabwe suspended from Commonwealth.

National Political & Socio-Economic Context	Civil Society Context	National Machinery & Policy Context	Women's Movement
• Draft constitution compiled amidst furore over accountability[13] and transparency of the process. • A referendum on the constitution is held early in 2000 and results in a historic 55% "no vote" in rejection of the CCZ draft constitution and the first ever-electoral reverse and defeat of ZANU PF. • Campaigning for General Elections takes place amidst politically motivated clashes between ZANU PF and MDC supporters. • War Veterans supported by the State begin their reign of terror in seizing white commercial farming lands ostensibly to redistribute the land. • Operating from these bases they waged war on commercial farmers and opposition activists. Loss of life, destruction of property and crops, rape and assaults. The police did not intervene. • Total collapse of the rule of law and gross human rights violations.	• The Zimbabwe Congress of Trade Unions announces its intent to form a political party.[14] • The Chairperson of the NCA resigns to be replaced by the vice-chairperson, an activist from the women's movement. • The Movement for Democratic Change (MDC) is formally constituted as a political party spearheaded by workers and launched with the slogan "chinja" or change. • The NCA process to produce a draft constitution runs parallel with that of the CCZ. • NCA calls for a no vote and campaigners are subjected to violence as opposition groupings clash. • MDC Campaigning for elections begins. • Politically motivated violence breaks out in the lead up to the elections. Clashes between MDC and ZANU-PF supporters. • It becomes too dangerous for the MDC to campaign in parts of the country.	• With limited resources and even less political will gender reduced to window dressing has not been undertaken with any meaningful commitment or subsequent result. • National Gender policy Programme launched by MNAECC in 1998. The Ministry employs gender consultants to work on the drafting of the policy. • Zimbabwe governmental delegation presents a glowing report on its implementation of CEDAW to the CEDAW Committee in New York.[15] • The presentation of this report was delayed due to what the Ministry termed 'financial and administrative issues.' • After a fraught process a draft gender policy is completed in late 2000. • The post-election cabinet sees the dissolving of the position of Minister of Gender in the President's office. • Rather a new Ministry: Youth, Gender and Employment Creation is formed.	• Women's Coalition on the Constitution[16] is formed. • Land lobby group is formally constituted through an NGO – The Women and Land Lobby Group concentrating on securing land rights for women. • Women from the movement appointed as commissioners of the CCZ, similarly NCA National Assembly in 1999 elects 8 women out of a total of 18 members. • Women's Coalition embarks on campaign that shifts the focus from the NCA and CCZ to women themselves.[17] Tensions appear when women realise the need to take a side. This surfaces in their differing aspirations and results in argument and suspicion over the way forward. • Women decide to call for a no vote and march against the CCZ draft constitution to mark the beginning of their "vote no campaign". • Ushers in politically motivated violence against women as they challenge the state.[18] • Women from the movement prepare to stand as MDC candidates for election.

Snapshot of the Period (1995 – 2000)

Global trends
N/A

National Political & Socio-Economic Context	Civil Society Context	National Machinery & Policy Context	Women's Movement
• Mid-2000 elections sees a historic unsettling of ZANU PF, who secure 62 seats, 51.7%. • The 9 months old MDC secure 57 seats, 47.5% out of a total of 120 seats.[19] • Instability intensifies mass emigration of Zimbabweans regionally and internationally. • Land Invasions translate into speculation of food shortages and reduced foreign currency exports in 2001. • The State manufactures a race war as black, white and Asian Zimbabweans are pitted against each other. This is openly supported by the state that begin to blame racial groupings for the socio-economic and political scenario.	• Civic leaders, academics and members of the private sector launch IDEAS which is to serve as a think tank initiating public debate, policy evaluation, • Advocacy and information sharing.	• The Ministry of Youth, Gender and Employment Creation focuses upon amongst other things: economic empowerment of women, women in decision making, the domestication of CEDAW and the institutionalising of gender desks in line ministries.	• A Women's Election Network (WEN) is formed,[20] in preparation for the elections and to strategise against the prevailing male status quo. • Women are the victims of targeted state sponsored violence and intimidation prior to elections. • Elections see a total of 13 women MPs elected, a drop from the previous term.[21] • The politicisation of the movement results in a backlash. Long-standing women's organisations come under threat and experience a weakening by conservatism both internal and external. • In the face of increasing politicisation it opts to 'lie low' until after the Presidential elections of 2002.

Snapshot of the Period
Endnotes

1 Demonstrated move away from previous welfare approach through newly established NGOs focussing on: environment, human rights, gender, health including HIV- and AIDS-awareness, prevention and reproductive health, business support.

2 NGOs convened the first meeting of its kind in Murewa in 1996 to discuss the need for collective advocacy/focus groups on key thematic issues i.e. poverty, land, and economics. These hubs were formed and were responsible for co-ordinating NGO activities and action within the thematic area.

3 MNAECC & UNDP (1997). Annual report: Women in Politics and Decision Making Project. Harare

4 The Act's major provisions set out the legal requirements relating to: 'The definition of organisations falling under the act and their activities, legal procedures for registering NGOs and selection and respective functions of the Minister, PVO Board and PVO registrar in the registering, monitoring and deregistering of NGOs'.

5 The PVO act signalled the eagerness of the state to control the growing NGO sector at a time when its political legitimacy was being increasingly undermined by growing economic chaos.

6 Educational strategies of the NCA also extended to a rural education programme, newspaper, radio and television. Initially the state refused to flight the NCA'S advertisements on the grounds that the latter was a political party. The NCA challenged the legal basis of this prohibition and won. However the state-controlled media still remained reticent in airing NCA material.

7 The group, the first of its kind in Zimbabwe and perhaps the region, challenged men to contribute to national development by engaging with gender issues. 'We have analysed and noted with concern the problem of gender inequality as a moral and political challenge. Our society continues to promote a culture and attitudes based on domination and exploitation of women by men.' Jonah Gokovah, Chairperson Padare, 1999.

8 The two ministers, heading the MNAECC and the younger Minister of Gender seemed to embody and surface tensions and generational undercurrents which were a microcosm of developments in ZANU-PF around alternative ways of governance, almost twenty years after independence.

9 The first attempt at consolidating and forming a permanent coalition of women took place in the form of the Women's Federation. Born out of discussion around the direction of the women's movement in 1995, it took two years before it was launched in Bulawayo. The two-year period was fraught with problems in trying to get the federation up and running, perhaps an indicator of a premature effort. The aim of the Federation was conceptualised as a pooling of experiences of all its members in building a common front and a power base to create a critical mass for asserting demands. The Federation was seen as providing a potential platform for solidarity from the draconian PVO act that women's groups were experiencing. It was envisaged as mass-based and mass-directed. The Federation did not take off, but was rather re-incarnated in the form of the Women's Coalition on the Constitution in 1999.

10 The government desperately needed to be seen to be doing something in the face of vociferous civic activism on the constitution.

11 The enormity of the task and challenges that confronted the CCZ were obvious at its inception, 20 May 1999. It was required to complete its work within six months and submit

a draft report and draft constitution by 30 November 1999 in time for General Elections in March/April 2000. The 395 commissioners were divided between nine committees, which formed the foundation and resource base of its work programme, the process, and the content that should become the new constitution. The most ambitious and pivotal outreach programme, involved some 100 teams and expected to hold 4,200 meetings across the country.

12   The NCA must be credited for bringing the debate in Zimbabwe onto the streets and to grassroots communities; its impact exceeded all expectations.

13   Consulting approximately 1/12 of the population, the draft was adopted without discussion by the commission. People wanted fewer presidential powers and more democracy, but the CCZ draft constitution disregards this view by enshrining ZANU-PF's grip on power, and allowing the President to run for two more terms with sweeping emergency powers.

14   Confirming the earlier fears of ZANU-PF politicians that the workers' umbrella body had a political agenda.

15   In the absence of governmental consultation and a masking of the truth, NGOs present a shadow report on the precarious position and condition of women in Zimbabwe to the CEDAW committee.

16   The Women's Coalition is a loose network of 66 women activists, researchers, academics, and representatives of 29 women's and other human rights organisations. It was launched in June 1999. It was initiated as a result of concern felt over the marginalisation of women and their issues in the two processes for Constitutional Reform (NCA, CCZ). The Women's Coalition was a response to a need shared by women's activists and women's organisations to create a platform that would unite women around the Constitution, provide information to women on the Constitutional Reform process, and the gender issues therein. It would constitute a critical mass for lobby and advocacy to engender the constitution-making process and ensure the adoption of a Constitution which protects women's political, social, economic and cultural rights.

17   Activities included one national and five provincial conferences to share information on the constitutional process, both NCA and CCZ, and to ascertain women's demands. A series of radio and television programmes, a video media campaign, lobby and advocacy materials i.e. posters, T-shirts, fliers, scarves etc. This process resulted in the production of a Women's Charter.

18   Reports to the coalition surfaced women being threatened, beaten and their property destroyed during campaigning.

19   Other parties comprised 0.8%. It was only by appointing an additional twenty MPs and relying on an extra ten, elected by pro-government traditional chiefs, that ZANU-PF was able to retain a clear majority.

20   Whose aim is the political empowerment of women. Bringing together women from all political parties including MDC and ZANU-PF. In the face of the 2000 parliamentary elections the organisation's main objective was to ensure that at least 40 women gained seats in parliament.

21   The Women's Coalition supported 55 candidates together with WEN. Six ZANU-PF women were elected and seven MDC women, amongst them women from the movement, human rights and grassroots activists. The President appointed two more women bringing the ZANU-PF women's representation to eight.

APPENDIX 2

Women Conversants

Maia Chenaux-Repond:
Then: Both Public sector and NGO experience. Advocate for women's land rights. Founder member of the Women and Land Lobby Group. Co-ordinator of the working group on gender politics. Consultant in the area of gender and development with Rudecon Zimbabwe.

Hope Chigudu:
Then: Senior researcher in the Ministry of Women's Affairs in the early 1980s. Founder and Board member of the Zimbabwean Women's Resource Centre and Network (ZWRCN). Consultant particularly within the SADC region.

Now: Renowned gender equality activist, consultant, and organisational development expert and strategist, she has supported a great many African and international justice groups, working in most African countries from Ghana to South Africa and serving on the boards of the Global Fund for Women and Urgent Action and on the working committee of the African Feminist Forum.

Sekai Holland:
Then: Active in the struggle for liberation from the late 1960s. Chair of the Association of African Women's Clubs. MDC candidate for Mberengwa East. Head of the MDC's international desk.

Now: Sekai Holland is currently the Zimbabwean Co-Minister of State for National Healing, Reconciliation and Integration in the Cabinet of President Robert Mugabe and Prime Minister Morgan Tsvangirai. On 30 April 2012, Sekai Holland was announced as the 15th recipient of the Sydney Peace Prize, Australia's only international award for peace.

Sarah Kachingwe:
Formerly permanent secretary in the then Ministry of Information, Posts and Telecommunications and a longtime advocate of women's rights, Sarah Kachingwe passed away on 7 June 2012. Before her appointment in the Ministry of Information, Posts and Telecommunications, Kachingwe was the Deputy Secretary in the Ministry of Community Development and Women's Affairs.

Nancy Kachingwe:
Activist based with Mwengo a regional reflection centre for NGOs. Portfolio includes

advocacy campaigns within civil society and advocacy, with specific focus on economic policy.

Pat Made:

Then: Rich experience as a GAD practitioner, journalist, writer and media trainer. Former director general of InterPress Services Africa. Board member of Women's Action Group and Zimbabwe Women's Resource Centre and Network.

Now: Currently, a consultant with UN Women in Zimbabwe. Board member of Gender Links, a regional NGO based in South Africa.

Shuvai Mahofa:

Then: ZANU member since 1965. Active participation in the liberation war. Instrumental in founding the ZANU-PF women's league. Member of Parliament since 1988 holding portfolios as Deputy Minister in both the Ministry of Women's Affairs and Political Affairs

Now: Deputy Minister, in the Ministry of Youth, Development, Gender & Employment Creation.

Revai Makanje:

Then: Legal advocate and staff member of Zimbabwe Women Lawyers Association. Co-ordinator of the Women's Coalition.

Now: Currently undertaking her doctoral studies with the University of Pretoria looking at women's participation and organising in political/legal processes of constitution making in Zimbabwe and Kenya. A member of the African Feminist Forum, and the African Network of Constitutional Lawyers, Revai has served on the boards of several women's rights organisations including feminist movement building organisation, JASS (Just Associates). She has worked for the Dutch development and funding organisation HIVOS, the United Nations Development Programme in Zimbabwe, and Zimbabwe Women Lawyers Association, engaging with civil society to challenge human rights abuses and gender injustice in Zimbabwe and the Southern Africa region.

Thoko Matshe:

Then: Feminist activist leader within the women's movement. Past director of the Zimbabwean Women's Resource Centre and Network and Executive Director of the National Constitutional Assembly. Founder member the Women in Parliament Support Unit.

Now: A committed women's rights activist and feminist, Thoko Matshe is the Africa Regional Co-ordinator of the Olof Palme International Centre. She sits on the board of several organisations, in South Africa, Crisis in Zimbabwe (SA) and Masimanyane Women Support Center, WIPSU (Zimbabwe), and internationally, the International

Feminist University Network and on the advisory board of IWRAW Asia Pacific.

Pat Mcfadden:

Then: Radical feminist activist. Academic co-ordinator of the gender programme at the Southern African Research Institute for Policy Studies (SARIPS), which is a part of SAPES Trust. Editor of the *Southern African Feminist Review* (SAFERE).

Now: Currently teaches, and advocates internationally for women's issues. Mcfadden has served as a professor at Cornell University, Spelman College, Syracuse University and Smith College in the United States. She also works as a 'feminist consultant,' supporting women in creating institutionally sustainable feminist spaces within Southern Africa.

Devi Pakkiri:

Lecturer in librarian science. Supported the development of the ZWRCN documentation centre and has served on the board of ZWRCN whilst continuing to be an active board member of WAG.

Rachel Simbabure:

Director of Gender, Ministry of Youth, Development, Gender & Employment Creation. Rachel Simbabure passed away on 9 May 2003.

Mary Tandon

Lawyer. Chair of Women's Action Group and member of the Zimbabwe Women Writers Association.

Iwani Tapela

Gender and development consultant and activist. Advocate for women's land rights. Member of the task force developing a National Gender policy. Commissioner to the Constitutional Commission of Zimbabwe.

Amy Tsanga

Then: Member of the faculty of law at the University of Zimbabwe. Co-ordinator of the Women's Law Centre at the University. Member of Zimbabwe Women Lawyers Association. Commissioner in the CCZ.

Now: Dr Amy Tsanga is the Deputy Director of the Women's Law Centre at the University of Zimbabwe. She is also a member of the Women's Action Group and the Chairperson of the Zimbabwe Women Lawyers' Association. She has been active in areas of access to justice, women's human rights and constitutional reform and particularly influential in the introduction of para-legals in rural communities. Amy has acted as a consultant to a number of international agencies such as UNIFEM and UNESCO and is Trustee for several NGOs, including the Swedish Human Rights Foundation.

Lydia Zigomo:

Then: Women's human rights lawyer and advocate. Director of the Zimbabwe Women

Lawyers Association. Chair of the Women's Coalition: Taskforce member of the National Constitutional Assembly.

Now: Lydia Zigomo Nyatsanza currently works as the head of East Africa region with WaterAid, an international development agency, focusing on provision of safe water and sanitation to the world's poorest communities working with local partners including national and local governments. She is also the equity and inclusion champion within WaterAid globally. Lydia has also been a core partner of the USAID Good Governance and Democracy Programme in Zimbabwe, an advisory group member of the UNDP's Conflict Transformation Programme for Zimbabwe, and chair of the Non State Actors Forum and of the EU / Zimbabwe Decentralised Co-operation Programme. Lydia is an Eisenhower Fellow (USA) and a former participant of the British Council Leadership Programme in Zimbabwe.

APPENDIX 3

Bibliography

Alexander, M.J. and C.T. Mohanty. 1996. *Feminist Genealogies, Colonial Legacies, Democratic Futures*. New York: Routledge & Kegan Paul.

Alvarez, S. 1990. *Engendering Democracy in Brazil: Women's Movements in Transition Politics*. Princeton NJ: Princeton University Press.

Amnesty International. 2000. Zimbabwe: Terror tactics in the run-up to Parliamentary Elections. London: Amnesty International.

Arnfred, S. 2001. 'Questions of Power: Women's Movements, Feminist Theory and Development Aid' in Sisak, A. (ed) *Discussing Women's Empowerment*. Stockholm: SIDA Studies No. 3.

Badran, M. 1996. *Feminists, Islam and Nation: Gender and the Making of Modern Egypt*. Cairo: Cairo University Press.

Barnes, T. 1991. Differential Class Experiences Amongst African Women in Colonial Harare, Zimbabwe 1935-1970. Paper presented at the conference: Women and Gender, University of Natal.

—— and E. Win. 1992. *To Live a Better Life: An Oral History of Women in Harare 1930-1970*. Harare: Baobab Books.

——. 1999. *We Women Worked So Hard: Gender, Urbanisation and Social Reproduction in Colonial Harare, Zimbabwe, 1930-1956*. Oxford: James Currey

Basu, A. 1995. *The Challenge of Local Feminisms: Women's Movements in Global Perspective*. Boulder: Westview Press.

——. 1992. *Two Faces of Protest: Contrasting Modes of Women's Activism in India*. Berkeley: University of California Press.

Bratton, M. 1994 *Civil Society and Political Transitions in Africa in Civil Society and the State in Africa* (eds) Harbeson J. W., D. Rothchild and N. Chazan. Boulder: Lynne Rienner Publishers.

Chigudu, H. 1997. 'Establishing a Feminist Culture: The Experience of Zimbabwe Women's Resource Centre and Network.' *Gender and Development*, 5 (1), pp: 35-42.

Davies, M. 1983. *Third World – Second Sex: Women's Struggles and National Liberation: 3rd World Women Speak Out*. London: Zed Books.

Ewig, C. 1999. 'The Strengths and Limits of the NGO Women's Movement Model:

Shaping Nicaragua's Democratic Institution' in *Latin American Research Review*, 34 (3), pp: 75-103.

Geiger, S. 1998. *TANU Women: Gender and Culture in the Making of Tanganyikan Nationalism*. Oxford: James Currey.

Getecha, C. and J. Chipika. 1995. *Zimbabwe Women's Voices*. Harare: ZWRCN.

Ghandi, N. and N. Shah. 1991. *The issues at Stake: Theory and Practice in Contemporary Women's Movement in India*. New Delhi: Kali for Women.

Haraway, D. 1991. *Simians, Cyborgs, and Women: The Reinvention of Nature*. New York: Routledge & Kegan Paul.

Harding, S. 1995. 'Strong Objectivity: A Response to the New Objectivity Question' in *Syntheses* Vol. 104 (3).

Hartley, J. 1994. 'Case Studies in Organisational Research' in Cassell, C. and G. Symon (eds) *Qualitative Methods in Organisation Research*. London: Sage Publications.

Hartsock, N. 1983. 'The Feminist Standpoint', in Harding, S. and B. Merrill and B. Hintikka (eds) in *Discovering Reality: Feminist Perspectives on Epistemology, Metaphysics, Methodology and Philosophy of Science*. Dordrecht: Reidel

Hassim, S. 1991. 'Gender, Social Location and Feminist Politics in South Africa' in *Transformation* 15.

Hellman, J. A. 1992. 'The study of new social movements in Latin America' in Alvarez, S. and A. Escobar (eds) Latin America and the question of autonomy in The Making of Social Movement in Latin America Boulder CO: Westview Press.

Jackson, C. and R. Pearson. 1998. *Feminist Visions of Development*. London: Routledge & Kegan Paul.

Jaquette, J. S. (ed). 1989. *The Women's Movement in Latin America: Feminism and the Transition of Democracy*. Boston: Unwin Hill Hyman.

Jayawardena, K. 1986. *Feminism and Nationalism in the Third World*. London: Zed Books.

Kandiyoti, D. 1991. *Women, Islam and the State*. Philadelphia: Temple University Press.

Lazreg, M. 1990. 'Gender and Politics in Algeria: Unravelling the Religious Paradigm', in *Signs* 15 (4) p 755-780.

——.1994. *The Eloquence of Silence: Algerian Women in Question*. New York: Routledge & Kegan Paul.

Legal Resource Foundation and Catholic Commission for Justice and Peace. 1997. *Breaking the Silence Building True Peace: A Report on the Disturbances in Matabeleland and the Midlands 1980-1988*. Harare: LRF/CCJPZ.

Mama, A. 1999. 'Dissenting Daughters? Gender Politics and Civil Society in a Militarised State' in CODESRIA Bulletin 3 & 4.

———. 2001. Bridging Legacies, Building Futures: Reflecting on African Women's Organising in the 21ˢᵗ Century. A paper presented at the Centre for Gender and Organisations Conference: Chasms and Differences. Simmonds Centre, Boston.

Mamdani, M. and E. Wamba Dia Wamba. 1995. *African Studies in Social movements and Democracy*. Dakar: CODESRIA.

Manuh, T. 1993. 'Women, the State and Society under the PNDC' in Gyimah-Boadi, E. (ed) *Ghana Under PNDC Rule*. Dakar: CODESRIA;

———. 1991. 'Women and their Organisations During the CPP Period' in Arhin, K. (ed). *The Life and Work of Kwame Nkrumah*. Accra: SEDCO.

Mba, N. 1982. *Nigerian Women Mobilized: Women's Political Activity in Southern Nigeria, 1900-1965*. Berkeley: Institute of International Studies at the University of California in Berkeley.

McFadden, P. 2000. 'The State of Feminism in Africa Today'. *Commentaries* 2, Nordic Africa Institute.

Mohanty, C. T., A. Russo and L. Torres. 1991. *Third World Women and the Politics of Feminism*. Bloomington: Indiana University Press

Molyneux, M. 1998 'Analysing Women's Movements' in *Development and Change*, 29 (2), pp. 219.

———. 1985. 'Mobilisation without emancipation? Women's interests, the state and revolution in Nicaragua.' *Feminist Issues*, 11(2); pp: 227-253.

Morgan, R. 1984 *Sisterhood is Global: The International Women's Movement Anthology*. New York: Anchor Press.

Moser, C. O. N. 1993. *Gender Planning and Development*. London: Routledge & Kegan Paul.

Moyo, S., J. Makumbe and R. Raftopoulos. 2000. *NGOs the State and Politics in Zimbabwe*. Harare: SAPES Trust.

Moyo, S. *The Land Question in Zimbabwe*. SAPES Trust: Harare.

Narayan, U. 1989. 'The Project of Feminist Epistemology: Perspectives From A Non-Western Feminist' in Jagger, A. and S. Bordo (eds). *Gender/Body/Knowledge: Feminist Reconstructions of Being and Knowing*. New Brunswick: Rutgers University Press.

Parpart, J. and K. Staudt. 1989. *Women and the State in Africa*. Colorado: Lynne Reiner Publishers.

Paul, E. 1993. 'The Women's Movement and the Movement of Women' in *Social*

Shemurenga: The Zimbabwean Women's Movement 1995-2000
Policy, 23 (4), pp: 44-51.

Ramazonoglu, C. 1997 'The Challenge of Local Feminisms: Women's Movements in Global Perspective' in Women's Studies International Forum', 20 (4), pp; 565.

Ranchod-Nilsson, S. and M. Tetrault. 2000. *Women States, Nationalism: A Home in the Nation*. London: Routledge & Kegan Paul.

Rai, S. 1996. 'Women and the State in the Third World: Some Issues for Debate' in Rai, S. and G. Lievesley (eds). *Women and the State: International Perspectives*. London: Taylor Francis.

Ray, R. 1999. 'Women's Movements in the Third World: Identity, Mobilisation and Autonomy' in *Annual Review of Sociology*, 25, pp: 47-50.

Reinharz, S. 1992. *Feminist Research Methods in Social Science*. Oxford: Oxford University Press.

Rowbotham, S. 1992. *Women in Movement*. New York: Routledge & Kegan Paul.

Rukuni, M. et al. 1994. 'Report of the Commission of Inquiry Into Appropriate Agricultural Land Tenure Systems'. Harare: Government Printers.

Schmidt, E. 1992. *Peasants, Traders and Wives: Shona Women in the History of Zimbabwe 1870-1939*. Portsmouth: Heinemann.

Sen, G. and C. Crown. 1987 'Alternative Visions, Strategies and Struggles' in Sen, G. and C. Crown (eds) *Development, Crises and Alternative Visions: Third World Women's Perspectives*. New York: *New York Monthly Review Press*.

Staunton, I. (ed), 1990. *Mothers of the Revolution*. Harare: Baobab Books

Stott, L. 1989. *Women and the Armed Struggle for Independence in Zimbabwe 1964 – 1979*. Edinburgh: Centre for African Studies.

Tamale, S. 1999. *When Hens Begin To Crow: Parliamentary Politics in Uganda*. Boulder: Westview Press

Tarrow, S. 1994. *Power in Movement: Social Movements, Collective Action and Politics*. Cambridge: Cambridge University Press.

Taylor, V. 'Gender and Social Movements' in *Gender and Society*, 13 (1), pp: 8-35.

——. 2000. *Marketisation of Governance: Critical Perspectives from the South*. Cape Town: DAWN

Tichagwa, W. 1998. *Beyond Inequalities: Women in Zimbabwe*. Harare: SARDC/ZWRCN.

Tripp, A. M. 2000. *Women in Politics in Uganda*. Oxford: James Currey.

Tsikata, E. 1989. 'Women's Political Organisations 1951-1987' in Hansen. E. and K. Ninsin (eds) in *The State and Development and Politics in Ghana*. Dakar: CODESRIA

——. 1999. 'Gender Equality and the State in Ghana: Some Issues of Policy and Practice'.

In Imam, A. et al. *Engendering African Social Sciences*. Dakar: CODESRIA

Vargas, V. 1991. 'The Women's Movement in Peru: Streams, Spaces and Knots' in *European Review of Latin American and Caribbean Studies* 50. pp. 7-50.

Vargas, V. 1995. 'Women's Movements in Peru: Rebellion into Action' in Wieringa, S. (ed) *Subversive Women: Women's Movements in Africa, Asia, Latin America and the Caribbean*. New Delhi: Raj Press.

Watson, P. 1998. *Determined to Act*. Harare: WAG.

Wieringa, S. (ed) 1988. *Women's Struggles and Strategies*. London: Gower Press.

—— (ed) 1995. *Subversive Women: Women's Movements in Africa, Asia, Latin America and the Caribbean*. New Delhi: Raj Press.

WLLG. 2001. Women and Land Lobby Stakeholder Workshop

World Bank. 1987. *Zimbabwe: A Strategy for Sustained Growth*. Southern Africa Department, Africa Region, Washington.

Yuval-Davis, N. 1997. Gender and Nation. London: Sage Publications.

Zimbabwe Human Rights NGO Forum. 2000, *Who is responsible? A preliminary analysis of pre-election violence in Zimbabwe*, Harare: Zimbabwe Human Rights NGO Forum.

Zwart, G. 1991. *From WID to GAD More than a Change in Terminology?* Harare: ZWRCN

ZWRCN. 1994. *The Gender Dimension of Access and Land Use Rights in Zimbabwe: Evidence to the Land Tenure Commission*. ZWRCN: Harare.

—— . 2000. *The National Machinery for Women in Zimbabwe: An NGO Assessment*. Third World Network: Ghana.

MINUTES OF MEETINGS

Minutes of the meeting of the Women's Coalition for the Constitution 7 June 1999

Minutes of the Core Group Meeting of the Women's Coalition on the Constitution, 26 April 1999

NEWSPAPERS

(not referenced in footnotes)

Press Release 7 March 1996 'Constitution of Zimbabwe Amendment (No 14) Bill' (inserted by Hon. E.D. Mnangagwa, Minister of Justice, Legal and Parliamentary Affairs). Statement of the National Democratic Institute Pre-Election Delegation to Zimbabwe issued in Harare 22 May 2000

The Sunday Mail, 10 December 1989.

The Financial Gazette, 29 February 1996; 11 January 1997; 17 July 1997.

—— 'Huge Payouts for Ex-Fighters'. 28 August 1997.

—— 'The High Price of Peace and Folly' 4 September 1997.

—— 'Mugabe Raises Stakes in DRC Crisis'. 10 September 1998.

—— 'Commissioner Severely Assaults Colleague'. 15 September 1999.

—— 'MDC Launch Sets Stage for Bruising Battle'. 16 September 1999.

The Mail and Guardian, 'Zimbabwe Focus: Racism Lingers, But Class Divides'. 3 March, 1999.

The Daily Gazette, 12 July 1994.

The Daily News, 'Women's Groups threaten to reject draft constitution'. 20 December 1999.

—— 'Women Rally Together to Boost Participation in Civic Issues'. 15 May 2000

WEB PAGES

1980. Report of the Constitutional Conference Lancaster House London September – December 1979. London : Her Majesty's Stationary Office. Available at: http://wanadoo.nl/rhodesia/lanc1.html

UNDP 1999. Human Development Report: Globalisation with a Human Face. Zimbabwe. http://hdr.undp.org/reports/detail_reports.cfm?view=598

2000. A Summary of the Main Features of the Draft CCZ Constitution: Some of the reasons why NCA campaigned for a NO Vote. http://www.nca.org.zw/html/fdraft/fdraft_summ.htm

1999. Zimbabwe Biz. On The Constitutional Trail. http://www.zimbabwebiz/magazine/11-1999/nov04.htm

Appendix 4
Supplementary Material

The Zimbabwe Women's Charter

Preamble

We, the women of Zimbabwe, as full citizens representing over half of the Zimbabwean people

Having contributed equally to the development of the nation throughout its history

Having contributed equally to the struggle for the independence of our nation

Having suffered oppression through patriarchy, custom and tradition, colonialism, racism, male-dominated totalitarianism and capitalism

Finding ourselves still discriminated against in all aspects of national life – legal, political, economic and social, cultural and religious

As workers in every sphere of national life

As the mothers of the people and of future generations

Claiming the birthright of every human being to have freedom and equality

Demand

- Constitutional, legislative and policy measures that actively address gender imbalances.

- Recognition of our role in the foundation and development of the country.

- Full and equal participation in all aspects of national life.

- Freedom from all oppression.

- Full and equal rights in the legal, political, economic, social and cultural framework of our nation.

- The removal of discrimination against women in all aspects of public, corporate and private life.

- Affirmative action where necessary to right the injustices of the past against women and to give women equal partnership in the future.

- Guarantee of safety of person and property and active measures to end violence against women.

- A plan of action, a time frame for implementation and a realistic allocation of national resources to fulfil these objectives.

Equality and Non-Discrimination

- Women claim full equality with men in all aspects of national life. Their right to constitutional, legal, political, economic and social equality is unalienable and indivisible. To achieve equality, the nation, in all its organisational aspects, must recognise the oppression and disadvantages women have suffered and rectify this imbalance through affirmative action policies. In addition, non-discrimination against women should be enshrined in the Constitution and in all domestic law as an unqualified, justifiable and non-derogable principle.

- The principle of equality between women and men should be addressed in all legislation and policy instruments and additional legislation developed to rectify the imbalances of the past.

- There should be a justifiable Bill of Rights in a new Constitution to protect human rights and this should include a clear and unambivalent statement on full equality for women.

- The government should not only legislate for but also promote equality in all aspects of the public, corporate and private life of the nation.

- Legislation enshrining any principle of inequality or any form of repression towards women should be immediately repealed or amended.

- Women should have equal rights within the family, equal rights to custodianship of children and equal rights in budgetary and family planning decisions.

- The equal right to basic livelihood is mandatory and to achieve this women demand full equality at work, equality amongst siblings in distribution of inheritance, equal right to land and equal right of access to other natural resources and capital. There should be appropriate legislation, allocation of resources and steps to monitor and implement this.

- Female and male family members must be accorded equal rights to inheritance, including inheritance of land and housing.

- Women have the right to housing, social welfare and education.

- The state has an obligation to educate its people on their rights to equality, both before the law and in all aspects of society.

- Measures should be taken to encourage the media to present positive portrayals of women that are not based on gender stereotypes.

- Women should be equally represented at all levels of local and national government and all policy-making boards and institutions.

- Adequate budgetary resources must be allocated to ensure equality and non-discrimination.

- Whilst fully respecting the role culture and religion play in family and all other aspects of life, these must not undermine the attainment of full equality between men and women in the public and private sphere.

- To ensure enforcement of such rights, a gender sensitive justice delivery system must be cultivated by the state to ensure that women can access their constitutional rights.

Law and Administration of Justice

- The principle of equality for all in areas and aspects of life, including national life must be supported, protected and advanced by laws that actively confer equality of rights and opportunities on women and the girl child. Equality for all must be supported by a gender sensitive and socially sensitive judicial and law enforcement system. All citizens must be able to have ready access to the appropriate court to enforce their legal rights and entitlements.

- Women must participate fully in local adjudication and mediation processes, there must be affirmative action to ensure that women are equally represented at all levels of the judicial process, in the administration of justice and in national law enforcement bodies.

- All laws and all government agencies should recognise, protect and enforce the right of women to an independent identity and her right to self-determination as an individual and to exercise her rights and duties as a parent.

- Measures must be implemented in the law and in the processes and procedures of the administration of the courts to ensure that all courts are litigant and victim friendly. This must be specially implemented for the benefit of rape victims, victims of domestic violence and victims of child sexual and other abuse.

- Special assistance and protection must be made available to those who are mentally or physically disabled when they engage with judicial processes whether as civil litigants or accused persons, witnesses or defendants in criminal cases.

- The judiciary must be an independent and autonomous body, composed of persons of the highest moral integrity and reflect gender equality.

- Women must serve on all courts, including customary law courts, at all levels as judicial officers.

- Affirmative action measures must be taken to increase the number of women serving as judicial officers in all courts until parity between male and female judicial officers is reached throughout the entire judicial system. For the avoidance of any doubt such affirmative action must apply to customary courts and all other tribunals.

- All judicial officers must receive gender sensitive training and all judicial officers must be trained and encouraged to deliver judgements that uphold women's rights and protect the rights and interests of women.

- For the effective enforcement of human, civil and legal rights legal aid and assistance services should be made available to all citizens who are unable to afford the services of a legal practitioner.

- To ensure that the judicial system and law enforcement processes are adequately funded and supported there should be a separate budget, voted annually by Parliament and provided for in the constitution to ensure that individuals, especially women, are able to effectively pursue their rights.

- The criminal justice system should be made more sensitive to the needs of women in cases of violence against women including domestic violence.

- Police officers must be compelled to, and receive appropriate training to ensure that they treat all persons equally, police officers must be trained to treat women with respect and as equal human beings to men.

- Police officers must be compelled to provide protection for women against all forms of violence and must be particularly obliged to take all possible measures to protect women from gender violence and to deal with victims of all forms of gender violence seriously and sensitively.

- All citizens must have free and full access to information regarding their legal and constitutional rights.

Property, Resources, Land and Environmental Rights

All women should have the right to full participation in the economy. Women have a right to employment, the right to own or occupy land in their own name and in their own individual capacity. Women and men must be regarded as having an equality of rights to matrimonial and family property. A clean and healthy environment, protection and equality of access to natural resources for women and men are fundamental elements in women's enjoyment of property and resource rights.

- Women must have the right to enter and pursue careers of their own choice.

- Women have the right to employment and all the necessary services and facilities required for their full participation in employment, including rights of advancement and promotion. To secure and protect these rights maternity benefits must be provided by the state and the employer, childcare measures and the provision of childcare facilities must be made a priority in all work places and communities.

- Women must have equality of access to credit and other facilities to ensure their full participation in the economic life of the nation. Women must be recognised as entitled to apply for and obtain such credit facilities in their own right.

- Government must provide special credit and loan facilities to enable women to enter the economic field.

- Women must have equality of rights to own, acquire and utilise agricultural, residential and industrial land on the same basis as men.

- Married persons must be deemed to have joint title and rights to land and joint rights to housing acquired by them.
- Women must retain rights over the product of their work, to control their own incomes and the sale of the produce from their labour.
- Government must institute a gender balanced, transparent, financially supported land resettlement programme. Such programmes must be supported by adequate information and support to enable women to apply for and obtain resettlement land.
- Women's rights to own and dispose of movable and immovable property must be clearly recognised and enforced. Any laws that continue to deprive women of such rights must be regarded as discriminatory and therefore unenforceable.
- The state must ensure the preservation of national and natural resources.
- Resources must be managed by the state and local communities so as to ensure that local communities and individuals benefit from those resources. Local resource utilisation must be designed, wherever possible to enhance locally economic employment and financial opportunities.
- Utilisation of resources must be carried out in a manner that does not degrade the environment.
- A clean and healthy environment must be created, protected and preserved for all citizens.
- Access to clean water, adequate and safe sanitation provisions must be available to all citizens regardless of where they live in Zimbabwe.

Culture and Religion

Cultural and religious practices that discriminate against women, either directly or indirectly must be abolished. Women must have full and free self-determination. Cultural and religious practices that deny or fetter women's rights to such self-determination must be treated as unenforceable and every measure taken to ensure that they are abolished or suitably modified to eliminate such discrimination.

- All cultural and religious practices that discriminate against women, whether in the public or private sphere must be eliminated by active legal, social and educational measures that are fully supported and funded by the state.
- All laws and policies that discriminate against women on the basis of their marital status must be abolished.
- The state must take measures to ensure that all form of marriage, including unregistered customary marriages are given equal recognition and confer equal rights on the parties to that marriage.
- Women have the right to freely choose their marriage partners.

- Partners to a marriage must be granted equality of rights in matters regarding the marriage or the family that is produced from that marriage.

- Women must have equality of access to matrimonial property with men, regardless of the form of marriage, be it under general law or customary law.

- Women are entitled equality of access to and guardianship rights over children to those of men.

- *Lobola/roora* must be regulated so as to ensure that it is not used to oppress women, it should be regarded as no more than a token of the relationship between two families and should have no bearing or influence on the rights of the spouses to a marriage to any rights or entitlements that may accrue within that marriage. Women, where labola/roora is exchanged between families must, as the mothers and nurturers of the bride be entitled to an equal share of the labolo/roora to that of the father of the bride.

- Women must have the right, and the state must actively support that right, to participate fully in the cultural, artistic and sporting life of the nation regardless of their cultural, ethnic or religious backgrounds.

- The state has an obligation to ensure that women with disabilities are afforded every opportunity to enjoy their womanhood, including educational rights and the right to participate in cultural and sporting activities of their choice.

- Women must have free choice over matters of reproduction and the regulation of their fertility regardless of the religious, cultural or ethnic considerations, this right of choice and the right to a family must be especially protected and advanced for women with disabilities.

Violence Against Women

Violence in all its forms is endemic in Zimbabwean society. In most instances violence against women occurs in the family or the community. Although there are legal provisions that guarantee protection of underage girls from statutory rape, they are not sufficiently protected within the family or community. There also appears to be a cultural acceptance of men assaulting their wives. Violence cannot be eliminated if it is narrowly perceived as a family or personal affair. Violence denies women the right to personal development, security, respect and dignity.

- Women shall be entitled to be treated with respect and dignity by help agents such as the police, medical staff, and counsellors.

- The police, prosecutors, magistrates and judges shall be provided with appropriate education and training in human rights and gender sensitivity to enable them to protect women effectively.

- Victims of violence should be provided with counselling service and shelter.

- Government should put in place public education programmes to sensitise women and men to the fact the domestic violence violates the basic human rights of victims.

- Legal provisions should be made which specifically define domestic violence as a criminal offence. Rape charges should be stiffer in cases where a victim is infected with disease.
- The definition of rape should be expanded to include marital rape.
- There should be legal protection for all women against sexual harassment, all forms of abuse and assault. Sexual harassment should be made a criminal offence.

Women and Governance

The participation of women in decision-making and governance is a human rights issue. Women should have the right to participate fully at all levels of political, civic and community life.

- Government and all political parties should ensure equal participation of women and men and also women's representation in all national and local legislative and decision-making bodies.
- Any strategies that seek to address power sharing between women and men should target all levels of public and private life.
- Awareness of women's political rights should be actively promoted.
- All political parties must establish a quota system and implement it within their structures and constituencies to ensure that equality of numbers is attained between female and male candidates who stand for leadership positions.

Education and Training

The education of all citizens is essential to the proper development of the nation. Under certain cultural practices, girl children have had disadvantaged access to education. The education of the girl child must therefore be a priority of the state and society. The state must also reprioritise its budgetary expenditures to the development of its citizens.

- Every child shall have access to free, compulsory and quality education. The state shall provide free education at least through secondary school.
- Free and quality pre-schools shall be established for the benefit of working mothers and the proper intellectual, emotional and physical development of all children.
- The state shall institute affirmative action programmes for higher education and training institutions to rectify the historical disadvantages of female students.
- Affirmative action initiatives should also be enacted for the hiring of female teachers and lecturers as well as administrators to ensure the equal and full participation by women in education policy-making and the management of educational institutions.
- Women and girls shall not be denied their right to education on the basis of sex,

gender, pregnancy, marital status, physical or mental disability or age. Child-care facilities shall be established in schools or training institutions for the benefit of the children of teachers and students.

- Female students shall not be restricted in their choice of subjects/courses on the basis of gender stereotypes. Appropriate measures shall be taken to increase the participation of female students in the fields of science and technology. Textbooks should also be revised to avoid gender stereotyping of women.

- Female students shall be protected from violence, including physical and sexual abuse and harassment, in all schools, universities and training institutions.

- Sex and human rights education shall be components of the curriculum from primary through secondary school, as well as in skills training and adult education programmes.

- Gender awareness training shall be included as part of the training of all teachers.

- The state shall promote the linguistic, literary and cultural integrity of African languages by designating the language of the predominant linguistic group of a region as the primary language of instruction.

Health and Reproductive and Sexual Rights

The most urgent and devastating health issue in Zimbabwe is the spread of HIV/AIDS. Women, especially poor women, are being infected at an increasing rate because of their disadvantaged political, economic and cultural status. The state and private sector must collaborate and take aggressive, immediate action in terms of providing: information about sexuality, contraception and STDs; affordable treatment for people living with HIV/AIDS; and free contraception to both women and men, including sexually active teenagers. However, because general and reproductive health is inseparable from the wider political, socio-economic context, the state must also empower women politically, economically and socially.

- Women and children have the right to free/affordable, accessible and quality health care. Women must have access to reproductive health and family planning services, including the right to information on sexual, reproductive and family planning matters.

- Women have the right to free/affordable maternal care, including prenatal, labour and post- natal care.

- Health care should be made responsive to the needs of disabled women.

- Women must have access to the full range of contraception free of charge. Women must also be provided information on the negative side effects of each form of contraception and be given the liberty to choose which method they want to use.

- Women have the right to control over their bodies and sexuality. Therefore, women have the right to choose their sexual partners, the right to decide on when and how often to have sex and the right to refuse sex, even within marital relationships. Women also have the right to decide when and how often they desire to have children.

- Women and children must be treated with respect and dignity at health and family planning facilities.

International Conventions

- All International Conventions promoting human and women rights that have been signed and ratified by the Government of Zimbabwe should be automatically incorporated into domestic law.

- The government should educate all people on the content of the international conventions. To facilitate the mass education campaign, the conventions should be translated into all the vernacular languages.

- The preservation of peace and declaration of war are aspects of international life which affect women profoundly and there should be mechanisms in place to ensure equal representation of women at all levels in any such decisions and negotiations.

Implementation Mechanisms

The national institutional mechanisms for implementing programmes to promote gender equality and women's rights and to monitor progress are not yet fully developed. Gender equality is not yet integrated into policies and development programmes and practices at all political, economic, social, private and public institutions.

- A Gender Commission should be established to guide, monitor and evaluate the implementation of legislation and policy in relation to women's and gender issues. The national budget should provide an adequate funding for the Commission.

- Measures must be taken to strengthen the capacity of those engaged in gender-focused research and to increase the production of gender sensitive information.

- Government, political parties, the private sector and civil society organisations should adopt the goal of bringing gender into the main stream in all aspects of their management, policies, programmes, procedures and organisational behaviour.

- Public interest litigation should be established to enforce women and gender rights.

- There must be a consistent gender audit of policies, budget and legislation.

- Measures must be put in place to ensure that sex and gender representations in the media are not of a discriminatory character with regards to women.